RIDDLE
OF THE
WAVES

RIDDLE OF THE WAVES

The Inspiring Story of Military Veterans Circumnavigating the UK

STEVEN PRICE BROWN

ADLARD COLES NAUTICAL

B L O O M S B U R Y

LONDON · OXFORD · NEW YORK · NEW DELHI · SYDNEY

Adlard Coles Nautical
An imprint of Bloomsbury Publishing Plc

50 Bedford Square
London
WC1B 3DP
UK

1385 Broadway
New York
NY 10018
USA

www.bloomsbury.com
www.adlardcoles.com

ADLARD COLES, ADLARD COLES NAUTICAL and the Buoy logo
are trademarks of Bloomsbury Publishing Plc

First published 2017

British Library Cataloguing-in-Publication Data
A catalogue record for this book is available from the British Library.

Library of Congress Cataloguing-in-Publication data has been applied for.

ISBN: HB: 978-1-4729-4576-1
ePDF: 978-1-4729-4578-5
ePub: 978-1-4729-4574-7

2 4 6 8 10 9 7 5 3 1

Typeset in Haarlemmer MT by Deanta Global Publishing Service, Chennai, India
Printed and bound in Great Britain by CPI Group (UK) Ltd, Croydon CR0 4YY

MIX
Paper from
responsible sources
FSC® C020471

To find out more about our authors and books visit www.bloomsbury.com.
Here you will find extracts, author interviews, details of forthcoming events
and the option to sign up for our newsletters.

For Margaret June and Suzanne

CONTENTS

INTRODUCTION:
THE CHALLENGE

THE IDEA WAS TO SAIL all around the UK on a tall ship, the ones that have no fancy modern winches or motors but instead give a whiff of times past when Britain ruled the waves and tattoos were worn by sailors rather than digital types sipping flat whites. The journey was to be called the Round Britain Challenge, a title that had been carefully considered. It wasn't a race, nor was it an expedition, the former throwing up a multitude of rules and regulations and the latter seeming a bit extravagant. It was to take place in the summer of 2016, and to start and finish at Falmouth, a quiet haven far down to the west of England and a place too far from anywhere to feel anything but quaint.

The ship was to be propelled by sail, and the sails to be raised and lowered with ropes or 'lines', at the end of which would be us, sweating. 'Us' was a group of military veterans, a ragtag bunch all with a common thread: we wanted to move on with our lives. We had changed from being sharp-seamed, uniform-clad warriors to hoody-wearing civilians and it had not been an easy transformation. We had all been involved in conflicts that had affected us and had tried to deal with them in our own way, usually unsuccessfully. Some of us had spent time living on the streets, others lying in hospital beds, many alone, some silently angry. Through various routes we had found ourselves sailing and it had proved to be incredibly restorative. More importantly, it had put purpose back in our lives. As military types we had the urge for adventure, and ideally it had to be foolhardy and brag-worthy.

The challenge was organised by the military charity Turn to Starboard, the brainchild of ex-RAF squadron leader Shaun Pascoe. Cornish born and bred, he set his charity up in Falmouth, a suitable home for this quiet, positive, capable man. He is one of those guys who enters a room silently, watches, listens and slowly engages, making you feel special, putting a metaphorical arm around your shoulder without compromising your damned macho ego. He wasn't a tall man nor one who relied upon his physical presence to narrate for him. Like almost all of us, grey hair had started to appear at his temples and more so in his stubble. Once you got to know him, his natural mischievousness would surface, but always accompanied by a softness. He was one of the good guys.

To be selected to come on the trip, there had been a process of a kind. The challenge would take two months and spending that time at sea would be a huge commitment: time away from loved ones, from family, from the safety of one's home, from routine, from the things that each of us had constructed around us to create a pleasant, or at least a livable, life. Then there was the matter of what you were letting yourself in for: fixed surroundings, no escape, living in close quarters with people suffering from the effects of time spent in warzones, who can find life hard.

In late 2015, emails were sent out to see who was interested. The first worry was that there wouldn't be enough crew. That worry subsided very quickly in the face of a huge response. Shaun took the decision that if you applied, you were selected, simple as that. As a charity they wanted to help as many veterans as possible, so everyone who showed interest was invited down to Falmouth for a three-day taster session of what they were letting themselves in for. Maybe he didn't realise it, but he seemed to have used the 'we don't leave anyone behind' mentality so often associated with the military.

We were split into three manageable groups for the briefings and the three-day acclimatisation sailing trips. Shaun gave the first two briefings. Everyone assembled in the teaching room, grabbing a hot drink, checking their watches, all making sure they didn't commit the cardinal sin of being late. Each person introduced themselves, some at length, others uttered their name and no more. Some were clearly more self-conscious than others. But when it came to the short sailing trips, all worked hard, helped to cook, kept their bunks tidy. I saw a few really embrace the task, keen to help whenever a sail needed raising. Some, naturally, found it easier than others.

For the last briefing, Shaun was away fundraising and asked me to stand in for him as I had now been kicking around for a few weeks. I had been living on the boat and was slowly picking up the gist of what was happening. I mumbled through my notes, but it was during the questions part that I got to see another unique aspect of this trip. This was to be a challenge for a team but an odyssey for the individual. Every single person had a place in mind as their own pilgrimage during the trip, somewhere they felt drawn to. Together we were going to visit the four corners of a nation that we had given solemn oath to defend. This was to be a cathartic process for a lot of lost souls, a freeing of shackles of the past. We were going to make lifelong friends and return more whole than when we left.

01
THE ANNIVERSARY

'My story starts at sea'

Shakespeare in Love

OUR COUNTRY IS SAFE. It is safe compared to other nations now and it is safe compared to our own nation hundreds of years ago. Our seas, however, will never be totally safe. The tall ship in which we were to pursue our challenge, the *Spirit of Falmouth*, is a replica of an eighteenth-century gaff rigged Mersey pilot schooner, which once guided tall ships into the dangerous waters of Liverpool Bay. Before that pilot service came into being, ships often attempted to sail into Liverpool without local knowledge and certainly no modern beeping machine to help when visibility was poor. It was a dangerous undertaking.

LIVERPOOL BAY, IRISH SEA, 1764

It was his body language first and foremost that let them know they were about to die.

The captain's control of the helm was normally so complete – a master caressing the ship's wheel, the wheel answering back with compliant squeaks. Generally he overemphasised the movements while adjusting the ship's course, a performance to show any onlooker his utter competence. It's the job of a skipper to give confidence.

But now everything was wrong. His oilies were wildly flapping open, the angry wind tearing at the bottom hem of his jacket as though to pull it right off his back. His heavy woollen jumper was soaked, still giving warmth but no longer protective. He was not guiding or steering any more. Roles had been reversed. The helm was juddering, snapping back, trying to knock him off balance, playing with him, flinging him around. It was all he could to hold on.

To his onlooker at first it was embarrassing, then comical: that moment when someone in a senior position loses their normal demeanour. Then the realisation set in. If he, the captain, was at the mercy of the helm, then they were all at the mercy of the sea.

These waters were famed for their difficulty and the ship was now on one of the worst parts, the Burbo Bank. This year alone there had been fifty wrecks with a death toll of fourteen people. The tide here was one of the most powerful in the sailing world. This port was lethal to negotiate.

Liverpool had always been a test of seamanship but with the recent increase in sea trade, supplying the demand for luxury goods, the traffic had grown and the timings had become more commercially important. Everyone wanted to be the one man who could 'bring it in on time'. Tall ships arrived daily completing the golden triangle of trade: slaves from West Africa to the Caribbean, sugar and cane to the British Americas, luxury goods to the UK.

As ship's boy, he only watched. He had not earned his say as yet. He was the greenhorn who was embarking on a long apprenticeship. It hadn't been his idea; his Ma had organised it.

'You'll thank me later, when you're prancing around, the new captain on the dock, all the girls aflutter,' she promised.

To get him here, she had spoken to one of her friends who worked at McCrady's, the local tavern, who had put the word around, using her big personality to swing the deal and get the boy a chance. A dinner had been organised and this large brutish man had sat where Pa used to sit, his Pa who had been lost to the sea. The stranger sat eating his huge meal, looking thoughtful; whether assessing him or his mother the boy'd never know. But later that month he had been called to the harbour office to fill out forms, and now he was aboard.

They had spent months at sea, visiting places that had overwhelmed his senses, testing the mind and the flesh. He had seen the coast of Africa, the sweet smells and tastes of the ports there. He had been with his first woman, paid for by a drunken quartermaster, who gave him a wink afterwards. The rolling seas of the Atlantic, where you could look all around you and not see any land, reminded him of the stories his father would recount on returning after months at sea. Huge sea creatures off the port bow, spouting water many feet into the air. Then the heat and paradise of the Caribbean, home of the famed pirates that terrorised the area.

But all that was in the past. Now they were in local waters where the ship was being pounded, fore and aft.

Soon after arriving into the British Isles, they had pulled into an island off the north Devon coast. Rough men with dark looks had unloaded some of the cargo. They carried on from there to Liverpool. It was the first job for many of this crew; some were novice sailors while others were just happy to be employed, to have a place to sleep and the company of like-minded men.

The trip across the great ocean had been simple but the final leg had been very different. As the ship had turned into the estuary a few things had happened that changed the normal routine. The most forward sail, the gib, had somehow worked itself free and landed in the water. Such a huge amount of wet canvas acted like a brake and the ship had heeled right over. While those on deck struggled to retrieve it, down below the cook was badly scalded from a falling pot spilling hot water.

The heeling had shifted all the cargo over to one side, so they then had to heave to and spend several days restacking, which put them behind. The captain had decided to make this up by ignoring the usual plan to approach the port only in daylight hours. It was summer but the light had faded and now they were approaching in the dark. Because of the all-hands call to work on the cargo, the watch rota had failed and the crew were exhausted. The swell had grown, the waves had slowly built and the boat rolled uncontrollably in force 10 winds. Sea spray whipped the deck. The boy on deck tried so hard to keep his reddened eyes open when he wanted desperately to close them.

They were sailing into trouble, in the dark, a novice crew, all working beyond the level of sense, all for money. As the boat rose up one side of a wave and down another, the ship twisted slightly, rolling, but the wind was incessant; there was no hiding from it. It was lashing from left to right, while the tide was fighting the opposite way. Ducking and bobbing between these two heavyweights was their fragile little New-York, an American gaff rigged schooner. The wind, their propulsion, their reason for existence, could never truly be harnessed. It was an uneasy partnership, a relationship set up to fail when one partner was as wild as nature. They had offered the primal wind too much of the sail. The wind squalled and caught the other side, tearing the mainsail across, gibing and creating huge forces while twisting the mast. The preventer, the rope to stop the swing, snapped, then came a huge oaky crack, a sound between a lion's roar and a crash of lightning.

The ship heaved to one side, water spilling on to the gunwales, washing the deck detritus away. The extreme pitch of the boat was too much for the cargo once more. Noises erupted from the hold. From the sliding and crashing sounds it was easy for the boy to imagine what was happening. The added weight to one side kept the boat at an angle, which in turn allowed more water to encroach. Finally the searching finger of the sea found the hatch to the hold, the water poured in and the boat slowly began to be engulfed. The end was close.

'To the boats, to the boats,' bellowed the captain at his wheel.

The lifeboats had been stowed on the port side to allow the speedy unloading at Lundy, the island they had stopped at, that illegal stop to put off some cargo to sell, the proceeds to be split among the crew. Since that stop had been made with great haste, the lifeboats had never been repositioned. They were secured but now half submerged. The first mate and bosun were each taking turns to go under the water and try to release them, using blades to cut away at the lines. The bow of the first lifeboat came free just as a wave crashed and twisted it on to the mate, crushing him against the mast, his hand still holding a knife but his wrist mangled.

The skipper was now next to three small crew who pointlessly pulled against the second lifeboat. The bosun tried once more to release the stern ties, then gasped as he rose out of the water, the lifeboat free. The remaining crew, *plus a shivering greenhorn, leapt into the wooden escape boat and rowed furiously for 20 to 30 feet, then turned to watch the* New-York *succumb. Allowing the water to take her, she silently disappeared below.*

The sea approaches to Liverpool, from the Irish Sea to the River Mersey, have always been difficult waters to navigate. In the early days of the port, visiting ships relied on local fishermen for skilled local guidance and assistance. However, with the expansion of foreign trade in the eighteenth century, the need for an organised service became apparent. In 1764 alone eighteen ships were wrecked in the Liverpool approaches and seventy-five souls were lost. The following year local gentlemen, merchants and tradesmen met at the Liverpool Exchange to consider the issue. As a result of their efforts, an Act of Parliament was passed in 1766 to establish the pilotage service. With the 250th anniversary coming up in 2016, Liverpool decided to commemorate the event with a festival, and pride of place was reserved to the replica pilot ship owned by the charity. Sailing *Spirit of Falmouth* back to the port in time for the celebrations would be a wonderful climax to the festival and a high point to our challenge.

To sail a ship designed in the eighteenth century into waters that had cost the lives of many far better seamen, men like those who lost their lives on the *New-York* and whose wreck still lay below the waves of Liverpool, was going to be a real adventure.

Falmouth was the perfect place to start and finish the challenge: just big enough to put on a show, and with its own, long maritime history. The high street was awash with maritime types wearing sailing boots and 'oilies' to keep out the rain, blue-hooped polo shirts and wraparound sunglasses. Every famous seafarer had one time or another ended up here, from Drake and Nelson to Macarthur and Ainslie. Falmouth was also home to the charity Turn to Starboard, whose name arose from the nautical term for turning towards the right or making a right turn, hinting towards positivity and recovery. The charity had been working magic with retired veterans. The word had spread.

Shaun Pascoe was a veteran. He had worked as the battlefield version of a paramedic. After many years involved in the mud and guts of warfare helping wounded soldiers, he had started his charity to help other veterans. He found that sailing had helped him recover, and from there the idea had blossomed. After two years, from an organisation based in his lounge and going sailing with a few mates, the charity had been gifted two boats and now employed eleven people, eight of whom were veterans needing the cure, plus three civilians to keep the madhouse in order. The charity was a focus-point of good sentiment from local people, who helped find – among other things – homes and clothing for the veterans.

Turn to Starboard didn't just take people sailing. It taught them how to sail, and to a very high standard. In fact, it could educate you to the standard of yachtmaster and then, if you wanted, it helped you get a job in the maritime industry.

The two biggest hurdles to an effective and successful charity are getting money and finding benefactors, so the Round Britain Challenge had been conceived to be a platform for both. It enabled the charity to engage with national media to get the message out there, appeal to the generosity of patrons, and most of all to find that guy or girl, get them off the sofa and on a pathway towards a more fulfilling life. That all sounds tickety-boo, but it takes a lot of organising, all from the offices in the marina.

Falmouth Marina looks very modern. The main building gives off a feeling of Portakabins. Not that it's temporary; maybe it's the metal staircases and balconies that rattle when you walk on them that create the effect. It is a squat, two-level building packed full of services: hairdresser, restaurant with obligatory bar, small chandlers, sail-training centre, boat sales, even financial advice and a chiropractor if things get a bit too much. And, of course, the charity.

After decades of wars in Ireland, Kosovo, Sierra Leone, Iraq, Afghanistan, and many other countries, the toll of combat and military service was starting to show. There will always be wars, there will always be soldiers, there will always be casualties, but this short period of relative peace with no major military involvements had allowed those services to take a deep breath, both as individuals and as a whole, and to have a look at what condition they were in. Since 2007 many new military charities had sprung up, all with great intentions but in some cases better intention than effectiveness.

Operations had ceased in Afghanistan in 2014; since then came the back end of the story. The more obviously wounded, such as the amputees from improvised explosive devices (IEDs), had mostly been dealt with and we had moved into the dark period of so-called 'hidden wounds'. This was the time when all those who had 'seen things' would struggle to deal with normal life, would go a little bit cuckoo and cause all around them to suffer.

One veteran recalled this conversation with his little son:

'Daddy, why are you going away?'

'Well, Daddy has to go and get his war madness cured,' the veteran replied.

The little boy looked up and off to the left as he no doubt recalled many memories.

'Mummy and I would like that,' he said finally, and nodded.

Many of us had managed to contract war madness and needed curing. For many, that was where the problems had started. There is no magical injection to be administered by a pretty nurse, or even by an ugly one. Most of us would let a disease-ridden leper give us a needle in the eye if it meant a cure. But the injection didn't exist and, to make the situation worse, it is unofficially accepted within military circles that anyone who is affected mentally is weak, so it would have to be a very cold day in hell before anyone would be admit to it. Many different types of physical and mental injuries had brought us, in different ways and means, to the beautiful seaside town of Falmouth in search of a tangible cure.

The charity's office is on the top floor at the marina. On the wall, just as you walk in, is a board that shows the family photographs: all the trustees and staff members. The veterans get a passport-sized photo too. Sailing is dynamic, so almost all the pictures are of gruff, bearded types, out there challenging the elements, oozing capability and masculinity. The photos are two-dimensional, as are the messages they tell. You need to talk to people to learn their story. Perhaps it's only fair if I start off with my own.

My Story

I was born in southeast London, the land of secondhand-car salesman and bank robbers. I had a sister Suzanne, six years older, and we had a good childhood together. She was a great sister and she really looked after me. We'd go on holiday to the Isle of Sheppey to my grandparents' caravan. I thought it was the sea when it fact it was the Thames Estuary, but a muddy beach was all the same to me. In the evening the residents would go up to the clubhouse and after a while there would be tables full of the old glass pint jars and a ceiling of smoke above everyone's heads. It was all very Chaz and Dave. I'd run around getting my head ruffled and cuddles from drunken aunts and uncles.

My parents were both Londoners. My dad's family were from Deptford and were dockers, while my mum's family were Irish and felt themselves a cut above. I always wanted my dad's mum to babysit because she was less strict and would give me chocolate and make me nice sandwiches.

After taking the eleven-plus I went to the same grammar school my dad and sister had gone to. It was a good school right bang in the middle of Deptford, and when the local comprehensive lads would see me at the bus stop with my little cap and blazer there would be a few scuffles. Guess that was normal in them days.

I didn't really get on with my dad. It seemed nothing was ever enough. I'd be captain of the football team and score five goals and he would tell me that at the same age he had scored ten. I ended up deputy head boy and captain of pretty much every sporting team, but he never said, Well done. Even after Prince Edward pinned my Afghan medal on my chest, Dad spent the rest of the day telling me how hard it had been during his peacetime national service.

But I've forgiven him now. His upbringing in a post-war inner city was awful. He has dementia now so we'll probably never get to have that normal father–son relationship.

When I was fourteen we moved out of London to Somerset, which was a hell of a culture shock. I rocked up with my snazzy London rig while they were all wearing DMs and tight black jeans. The deputy head stopped me in the corridor on my second day at school and asked me for my knife because 'all the kids from London carried knives'.

I got asked questions like, 'Did you know milk came from cows and not bottles?'

Then my sister got killed in a car crash. To be honest, I don't think I ever recovered from it. I adored her.

I did my A levels then for a while I did archaeology at university, but it bored me. After that I became a bit lost and a bit of a tearaway. I had a few scrapes with the law for minor things, and when I was old enough I went travelling. First to a kibbutz, then all across North Africa, working on digs as I was still interested in ancient ruins – Egypt was incredible for that – then I island-hopped in the Mediterranean before spending a while in Southeast Asia. I also hitchhiked across the US. I finally came home after a few years, got my hair cut, decided to be normal and got a job. I took the first job I could, which was in a warehouse, stacking boxes. Ironically the boxes were full of Dr Marten boots, a reminder of my schooldays. Anyway, this was now my career. For the next fifteen years, shoes it was. I got promoted a few times, ending up working in international sales, travelling with someone else paying.

Then I started out on my own, selling brands, made money, lost it, made money again, lost it. Fashion was as mad as music, loads of failed rockstars, and I fitted right in until one day it just didn't make sense any more. All I could see was how vacuous it was. I sold my business to a partner, downsized from a swanky London flat to a student house-share and mulled over my next move. All I knew was that I wanted it to be altruistic. I was 41 years old.

I wanted to do something medical. In fact, ideally I wanted to work for Médecins sans Frontières, the sexy medical charity that does all kind of good work in dangerous places. But seven years training to be a doctor or five years for a nurse seemed a bit too long at that age. I'd be geriatric before I got to do anything. Anyway, somehow I got to know that I could get medical training in the Army, so that's what I did. I joined up. Yes, I could do that at my age, but only in the reserves.

I got all the brochures for the different roles. The Royal Logistics guy had a hard hat, so that didn't look too much fun. The Medical Corps guy was a doctor with epaulettes. But the Infantry looked warry as fuck. So that was that. I joined the London Regiment, got on with the training and passed out in 2011. I signed up to tour with the Grenadier Guards in 2012 on Operation Herrick 16 and flew to Afghanistan in April. While the rest of the country enjoyed the Jubilee and the Olympics, I was in a dusty foreign land. We did four months ground holding from little check points and taking over compounds in the Upper Gereshk Valley, then two months based in MOB [Main Operating Base] Price doing strike operations. It was my one and only tour, so I have nothing to compare it to.

Out of our multiple of twelve men we had two double amputees, one gunshot wound to the face and one blast injuries to the face; luckily all survived. That's not counting the injuries received by the Afghan army guys fighting alongside us. Other platoons had it bad if not worse. Two of my best mates got injured by grenade.

I got my wish to be a medic. When we didn't have any designated med guys with us I was the platoon medic. Be careful what you wish for.

On one early morning patrol my mate Jay got hit by an IED [Improvised Explosive Device] and lost both legs. I treated him as well as I could. I remember holding his shattered leg off the mud and hearing him screaming while we cas-evaced him through the poppy fields and put him on the chopper thinking he was going to die, his injuries were so horrific. I can still remember the leg feeling like raw steak and the smell of burning flesh, and all the while he was choking blood from a huge hole in his throat. It was only when I got back that I knew he had survived.

That memory of his shattered body was the last thing I thought about before going to sleep and the first thing I thought about on waking up for many years.

He's OK now, though, and an inspiration to us all.

I got the last R&R window after four months of being in Afghanistan. I was sitting on the designated helipad waiting to start the long journey home when the flight sergeant appeared across the way and did the universal throat-cut sign: it's cancelled. I trudged back. I was off the rota so I volunteered to be guard commander for twelve hours until the next chopper.

During that period I ended up having to deal with another casualty, yet another double amputee. I say me, but it was a team. I just happened to be the guy in the wrong place at the wrong time, the one-eyed man in the land of the blind. A fellow Afghan soldier had been injured by a Taliban roadside bomb and had been brought to our base for medical assistance. We put him on a gurney bed and went to work putting tourniquets on his bloody stumps, but he was grey in colour. He had the normal Afghan bearded face, which was full of his own sick. As I felt him slipping away I gave him mouth to mouth, trying not to gag and pressing on his chest to give him breath. But we had got him too late; he died in my arms. I will never know if I could have done something else to save him.

The CSM [Company Sergeant Major] said to me, using my nickname, 'Unlucky, PB. Better get back to guard commander duty.'

By this time the Taliban were past masters at IEDs. We had a pick-up truck turn up one day. In the back were six kids. The Taliban had mistakenly blown them up while they were playing. The lads tried to save the ones who were still alive, who were screaming, while trying to match the body parts of the dead ones.

On shitty days, stuff like that doesn't leave you. But I know now that this was a normal experience for all those who had gone before and all those who came after me in Afghanistan. The chopper finally came and I got my R&R.

I came home in October 2012. I remember sitting on the tube in London, among all the commuters and the tourists there for the Olympics, me with my crisp, clean uniform but blood still on my boots, whether it was from Jay, the dead Afghan soldier, or one of the many kids, I couldn't remember. I knew I had had enough. I did the parades then left.

I was due to continue TA SAS selection, as I had been doing that before deploying, but as the mate I was doing it with had been blown up I kinda didn't fancy it any more. My head wasn't in it so I never would have passed.

I went to Kenya for the wedding of a Kenyan I had served with and while I was there I got a job working with an outdoor adventure company. I fell in love with the place and thought it would be the perfect environment to let the war seep away and get on with my life. For about a year it was fine. Then things started to change. I started getting short-tempered, anxious all the time, stressed over everything. I couldn't deal with people so I started to become more and more of a recluse. I got short of funds and did some private security work in Northern Kenya and South Sudan, doing what I had originally wanted to do: looking after aid workers in war zones. It was the worst thing I could have done. It made me more anxious and hyper-vigilant. I ended up a mountain, screaming at no one and going cuckoo. This wasn't the Steven I or my friends knew. I was out of control.

My friends paid for a ticket home.

Through Veterans Aid I got a place in the hostel in east London. About a month after I got back, my precious mum, Margaret June, died. Sweet and curious, she was forever reading accounts of derring-do, normally while sitting in her favourite chair wearing the pair of inappropriately fashionable trainers I'd bought her for fun. She had been unwell but had kept it from me. I got to spend a few hours with her before her death. I think she had hung in until I got there so she could say goodbye. She was high on drugs with the cancer eating away at her, but she had this moment of clarity moments before she died:

'I've always been so proud of you. When I gave birth to you I wanted you to go and see all that life has to offer, but when I looked in your eyes when you got back from the war, I knew you had changed.'

I was broken again. I had adored her but I couldn't even go to her funeral. I couldn't face it so I spent the day in the gardens of the Help for Heroes building in Tidworth. I made a vow to take any chance of adventure that was thrown my way. One day I got an email from Band of Brothers, the Help for Heroes charity, offering a sailing trip. I knew I had to do something so I wrote and got an email back pretty quickly telling me I was accepted.

Shit. I didn't want to reply, but I did. I didn't want to buy the train ticket, but I did. I walked around Falmouth for nearly three hours before I finally got the strength up to go to the boat. There I met some of the others and started to feel better, but I still kept my hood up to cover my face.

I loved the sailing. Turn to Starboard became my family, letting me stay on the boat, feeding me, giving me a focus, teaching me new skills.

Shaun has always helped people with more than just the sailing. He knew I liked to write so when the Round Britain challenge came up he invited me to participate and also to write a blog. That's where this book came from. It was just one of those things that escalated and I thought it might be a good way of giving back. It's a book my mum would have loved to read.

I'll never be able to repay enough.

02

THE SHIP

'You come of age very quickly through shipwreck and disaster'

Philip Dunne

SPIRIT OF FALMOUTH, a 92-foot, gaff rigged schooner, lay in Pendennis Marina. Huge thick lines attached her fore and aft to the pontoon. Car tyres and a crowd of differently sized and coloured fenders stopped her from banging against the pontoon and being damaged. Around her were luxury yachts, all buffed and pristine, preparing to depart to their winter homes in the Caribbean. *Spirit* was built in the 1980s, based on the plans of a real eighteenth-century Mersey pilot schooner, and was the last of her type. She has two tall masts, the taller being to the stern, the key element that makes her a schooner class. If the taller mast was towards the bow, she would be a ketch or yawl, which would affect her sail plan. So many wondrous words and phrases we learned. We all had such fondness for *Spirit* and such trust in her.

The first pilots to assist in bringing trade boats safely into port were fishermen who knew the waters and were given licences by the local harbour authority. As they were fishermen, their boats were slow, cumbersome, packed full of equipment and not designed for their new role. Some ports therefore developed pilot cutters, or single-masted sail boats. But others went one step further, adding two masts for a schooner. As usual, when it comes to things nautical, there are various rambling stories about the origins of the name, from *scoon* or *scone* in Scottish meaning a stone skipping across the water or from Dutch *schoen* meaning pretty or beautiful.

The schooner was designed and built for speed. Pilot ships would spot tall ships on the horizon and speed towards them. The first to arrive got the business and so speed and guile were paramount. When the new schooners started to display excellent speed, others came looking for the same benefits, including pirates. Schooners could be swift but they still had enough size to carry a few cannons to rain some terror down on their fat prizes.

We have to go back to the Thatcher years and the Liverpool riots of 1981 for *Spirit*'s conception and birth. The politician Michael 'Tarzan' Heseltine went to Liverpool with a big cheque book to stop the locals smashing the place up and find a few projects to give them something to do. At the time there was a regatta going on and so the idea was born of building a Merseyside pilot schooner in the dockyards using local unemployed youth on apprenticeships. She was always meant to be a training ship so there were a few amendments to the original design but generally it's quite close. Nothing goes up or down by anything but sweat.

Since then *Spirit* has been a beacon of youth development. She's had various owners and various names, *Spirit of Merseyside*, *Spirit of Scotland*, *Spirit of Fairbridge* and finally *Spirit of Falmouth*, but the cause remained the same. Now she looks after veterans, and is home to a few souls on a semi-permanent basis. When veterans first get involved with the charity they invariably end up staying on her for a few extra nights before or after the sailing trip.

Rich the bosun was one who lived permanently on the boat during the week. At the weekends he would travel back to his home in Plymouth. The winter swells can get a bit lively here in Falmouth marina, especially when there are strong easterlies, and *Spirit* lay exposed on the outer berth of the marina, taking the full brunt of the nautical attack. So when the waves grew, Rich would rouse all souls on-board and they would try as best they could to secure her against the inclement weather.

Rich was one of the real success stories. He had got involved with the charity via the military-support grapevine and his engineer skills were put to good use in slowly but surely getting *Spirit* back into a top-rate condition. Rich was 5 foot 9 inches, what he describes as the perfect height for a Royal Marine or 'bootneck'. He wore thick glasses, and used his obvious intelligence mostly for solving problems and displaying acute sarcasm. Everyone liked Rich.

So when you'd would get a nudge in your bunk, no one minded.

'Better give us a hand securing her or we'll be waking up in France or the seabed,' Rich would say calmly.

'OK,' you'd reply, half-asleep.

Night-time nautical emergency attire consists of wet-weather jacket, pants and boots. The pontoon could look quite camp. In fact, she looked like a pirate ship, appropriately enough.

'So, any ideas?' Shaun started the discussion. The chart of the UK was folded in half with just the southern half showing.

'Yeah, how about Gibraltar? That's got to be a fair distance,' offered Dan, an ex-marine, in his broad accent.

Dan had joined the charity as a beneficiary. A Yorkshire man, from Leeds, he had taken to sailing immediately and it had changed his life massively. He sported a beard for the past eight or so years, before they became fashionable, and it seemed to suit him. Thickset and powerfully built, his friends called him 'Silverback', but since I had met him he had only shown a heart of gold.

'Can't, the Mediterranean is non-tidal,' Fish replied.

Fish, aka Steve, was another bearded ex-Royal Marine who had now found a home with Turn to Starboard, a calm man, gentle and soft, with warm eyes and the patience of a saint.

The task was to find a mile-building trip for all the aspiring yachtmasters now affiliated to the charity. Shaun had his ticket, as did Fish. Dan was working on his yachtmaster and would have it before the trip started.

The only other in attendance was Tamsin, the only civilian in the group, who, although she was just in her mid-twenties, had more sea miles than everyone else combined. Tamsin was a local girl. Dotty about sailing, she ended up crossing paths with Shaun and he had noted what an asset she would be. He offered her a job, and since then this slight, utterly charming girl had proved to be more than even Shaun could have hoped.

'How far have you taken *Spirit* so far?' Tamsin aimed her question at Fish.

'West to the Scillies, east to Plymouth, but looking at her historical log, she's been all over the place.' He added, 'She is such a tart.'

'Well, isn't she in good hands, then?' Shaun joked.

Fish was the de facto skipper of *Spirit* and had been one of the first employees of Turn to Starboard. He arrived not long before The Prince's Trust gifted the *Spirit of Falmouth* to Shaun; that arose from a lucky meeting with Prince Charles at a garden function. Shaun had explained what the charity did and the prince had been so impressed that he had donated the ship to them.

To date, and to assist with the achievement of sailing qualifications, the charity had organised mile-builders to France, Guernsey and the Scillies, but those had been in a far smaller yacht. Even though *Spirit*'s size technically wasn't ideal for the RYA qualification, time at sea also counted. The yachtmaster qualification requires 2,500 sea miles, with a few more elements regarding night passages and pilotage.

'How about London, sail all the south coast, a busy pilotage coming into the Thames and a blinding night out when we get there?'

'Is London ready for you lot wearing dresses?' Shaun was referring to the Christmas party when all the guys came as the Christmas fairy. While he was doing that he used his thumb and little finger like makeshift chart dividers and estimated the mileage.

'It's six hundred miles there and back.'

'Dan, when you were looking into the accelerated programmes, how were they suggesting you get the mileage?' Tamsin as usual guided the conversation back to normality.

'Well, they suggested that –' he unfolded the map to show Great Britain in entirety – 'to sail all the way around the—'

Dan's and everyone else's eyes lit up. That's when the decision was made. No one from the team had ever done it before, 90 per cent of the crew would have had only a few days' sailing experience and, well, once you've started you have to go all the way.

Round Britain it was then.

But how was it going to be funded? Who was going to pay for everyone's food and drink, the fuel, harbour fees and all the other costs that would no doubt start to raise their heads once the 2,200-mile trip started to take shape?

International Paints is a global company that, funnily enough, is an expert in paints, including nautical ones. They had already enjoyed a relationship with Turn to Starboard and loved the idea of the trip around Britain. They were generous enough to offer a considerable amount to support the adventure. Problem solved.

In late 2015 the phone rang at the Falmouth office.

'Hi, my name is Stuart. I heard that *Spirit of Merseyside* lives down here now and has changed her name. I was involved with building her back in the 1980s and I wondered if it's OK to go and visit her,' the caller asked.

'Sadly I am away this weekend, but we have a veteran who lives on board, Steven. I'll get him to give you a call and you can sort out a suitable time,' Shaun answered.

That Sunday I was putting the kettle on in the galley when there was a knock on the hull. I popped my head out of the doghouse and there was a kindly looking man with bright eyes and a luxurious white beard.

'You must be Stuart. Come aboard, I'm just putting the kettle on,' I said.

Over the next hour or so Stuart walked me around *Spirit* and told me about this wonderful ship. Back in the day the original pilot schooners would paint a false bow wave on her, so that she was able to get just a few moments of headway before her competitors knew she was moving. He explained what colours she would have been originally, and that the gold line that ran from bow to amidships to stern had a key purpose. Customs officials made all the pilots have this painted on so they could keep track of the boats that needed to pay the taxes due from commercial ships. As if anybody would not want to pay taxes.

International Paints absolutely loved the idea of having the ship they were sponsoring taken back to her original colours. They would supply the material; we would supply the labour.

Rich's Story

I was born in Cornwall and raised on Dartmoor, so I'm a real country bumpkin. Me and my older brother were the tearaways of the village, setting fire to stuff, nicking stuff, selling stuff, scrumping, sticking our noses in mineshafts and so on. Even though he is older, my brother still gets ID'd. He's a lucky bugger. I reckon I must have had a tough paper round.

Our parents separated when I was a teenager. Mum raised us as Dad went off to France. It was tough for my mum financially so my brother and I left school to work and contribute. That's when we became 'entrepreneurs'.

My parents had always owned a boat, and in a weird *EastEnders* kind of storyline one of my Dad's best friends became my stepdad and started to teach me boat mechanics. They bought a boatyard and before I even joined up and then whenever I was on leave I would work there, learning and fixing stuff. Being in the forces was in the family: Dad was a submariner in the Navy and my grandad was a Para. I joined up when I was 16: the Army, the Royal Signals. I passed out on my seventeenth birthday.

I got trained as a linguist but very quickly I got bored. I wasn't doing any soldiering, which was what I had joined up to do. I told them I wanted to transfer to the Royal Marines, but they said I was too skinny and if I joined them I'd fail and it would be a waste of everyone's time. So I left anyway and went to live with my dad in the South of France for six months. When I came back I signed up for the Marines. It was 18 June 2001.

During our training, the directing staff came and told us that two planes had flown into the Twin Towers. No one believed them, but that's when the beat-up [mission-specific training] began for Afghanistan.

When you pass out in the Marines there is always a selection of roles available. I was asked if I wanted to be a chef, driver or signaller. I'd already been a signaller in the Army, I didn't want to be a chef, and I was mechanically minded, so I chose driver.

In 2003 at 20 years old I was sent to Iraq on Operation Telic 1. I arrived in theatre to be sent to join up with my unit and got put in the last vehicle of a convoy. We didn't have any maps or comms and got separated from the others. We went forward about two miles to try to find them but they weren't there, so we doubled back. Forty Commando were on R&R on the HMS *Ocean* in dock so we went there and got them to radio forward. The message didn't get through.

Apparently the padre was already on the way to my parents with the bad news when the call finally got through. The bloke running the convoy got a rollicking and I got praise as I had said I wasn't dashing over the border with just thirty rounds in my rifle, travelling in an unarmoured truck. I was MIA [Missing In Action] before I even started.

I got assigned to the EOD [Explosive Ordinance Disposal]. We were always blowing things up, getting rid of enemy missiles, making big holes in the ground, it was great.

My mum obviously thought I was in the movie *Saving Private Ryan* but generally when I got somewhere most of the action was over, though not always. I got used to the sound of incoming fire. I came home from tour and then went on exercise to the US, then Norway.

In 2009 my mum and my real dad died within ten days of each other. It was a tough time. It hit my brother hard and he went travelling for a year to try and make sense of it. He came back went to university and did a degree in film. He now works in Plymouth. He's got all the trappings, got married, has a dog.

In 2010 I went to Afghanistan on Op Herrick 14. I was now a mechanic tasked with fixing vehicles anywhere. We went to pretty much every FOB [Forward-Operating Base], MOB [Main-Operating Base] and a few CPs [Check Points].

When I went to Nowzad it was nicknamed Apocalypse Nowzad. The place was just rubble. We had Chinese 105 missiles and Soviet-made heavy machine-gun Dushkas to deal with.

At the time I was still enjoying it. Of course, it was scary, but when you are with your mates, it's funny how much you don't want to look a dick and so you just get on with it. After the deaths of my mum and dad I just wanted to experience as much of life as possible. I still do, though I know it can't always be good.

Not only did I lose my mum and dad, I also lost my stepdad, two uncles and a couple of friends, who hanged themselves after their experiences in Afghanistan, all within six months. That was full on. I tried desensitising with booze, drinking a bottle of rum or more a day so I was too drunk to even think.

I don't feel like I have PTSD. To be honest, I'd rather not get labelled with that, but I guess those who are don't want it either.

Then I got injured while on a junior command course. It was an eleven-week course: two weeks pre-course to shake out the dreamers, then nine weeks proper. I was doing a night navigation on Dartmoor. I'd already passed the course but we have a saying in the Marines that a C is a P, meaning a C grade is a pass, but I wanted to blow it out the water, maybe shake off the moniker of a REMF [Rear Echelon Mother Fucker; derogatory term used to abuse non-frontline soldiers]. But I fell a bit behind and changed my course to catch up. Anyway I fell off a tor, straight on to granite with a full 40lb pack on my back. Obviously the shock went straight through my spine. I got cas-evaced.

Next began a period of constant physio, but I got the feeling they thought it was all in my head. So I investigated it myself, paying for my own medical records, seeking loads of advice. I found a guy who would help and he and I worked out a suitable surgical fix. I went under the knife the day before my medical board, which would determine my suitability for continued service.

So I turned up, in clip [a really bad state], doubled over, almost licking my toecaps, in far worse shape than I would normally. I begged to stay, but it only took two minutes for them to kick me out.

After I left I tried one job in IT, but I told the boss it wasn't for me. I needed to be outdoors. I got involved with Turn to Starboard after seeing a banner at the Help for Heroes Endeavour Building in Plymouth. I went down to Falmouth and couldn't believe it when there were loads of bootnecks there. I volunteered for a while then Shaun offered me a full-time job looking after *Spirit*.

Working here and doing this has made me a better person. I work with vulnerable adults in a teaching role, running the deck, teaching navigation. Working with The Prince's Trust kids has been really good. I'm not so much a father figure, more a guiding figure, stopping a diet of gummy bears and energy drinks and showing them how to look after themselves. Yes, it's made me a better person.

03

THE BOAT SHOW

'Life is a gamble, you can get hurt, but people die in plane crashes, lose their arms and legs in car accidents; people die every day, you just don't let yourself believe it will happen to you'

Muhammad Ali

THE ARMED FORCES, whatever branch of them you serve with, love training, with good reason. They tend to send you to places where people shoot at you. While that's happening it makes a lot of sense if you know what you're doing, so the more you can be comfortable with being in the particular kind of environment the better. It's called mission-specific training and is part of your pre-deployment. In January 2016, one group were going to sail *Spirit of Falmouth* to London and another group would sail her back: a bit of mission-specific training for both greenhorns and experienced. The ruse was to arrive at the London Boat Show, dock outside, then spend the week there guiding the public around the ship, letting them know about the charity and passing the message to possible new benefactors.

This meant we had to get the *Spirit of Falmouth* to a fixed destination on a fixed schedule in winter conditions. For a bunch of novices it was a stiff ask.

Because it's on the tip of the Gulf Stream bringing all the warm air up from the Caribbean, Falmouth in January is a wet place. While the rest of the UK is trudging through sludge and snow, here it stays as rain. A few of the guys who had put their names down for the Round Britain had signed up for this trip. Fish would be skipper, Dan was first mate, Rich was bosun and Chris, an ex-army sergeant major who lived on the Isle of Wight, was a watchleader. Short and bluff with his words, brutally honest with his opinion, Chris was loyal, capable, yet completely unable to sit still. So, as the rest of the nation boxed up their Christmas trees and enrolled in three-month gym memberships, we got ready to sail.

With the lines pulled on deck, we were set. Six days' sailing to London lay ahead and only a few aboard had any idea of what that entailed. That said, if you wanted to choose a group of people with whom to wander into the unknown, with skills far below what was needed, then ex-service types are a fair choice.

As we got clear of the protection of Falmouth harbour, the sea waves hit us and three-quarters of us immediately turned green. There was not another sailing boat on the sea. We were joined instead only by floating mini cities of car ferries and oil tankers. It was a baptism of fire. The seasickness was debilitating. It's a condition whereby your world shrinks to the present time and to the state of your stomach. All you want to do is get off the boat and lie down somewhere that doesn't roll, or crawl up into a ball and swear to never, ever set foot on a boat again. I'd suffered from altitude sickness before, but this was like its far more powerful big brother.

Most of us had spent very little time on a boat before, but we did have in Fish a skipper who, while a veteran like the rest of us, had oodles of sailing experience, was a qualified yachtmaster and was as calm as a cucumber – at sea. On land he had an amazing ability to get blind drunk a few steps in to a pub and stay like that for the next eight hours, however much he consumed. We also had a few other experienced volunteers on board. Local sailing guru Pete Vandenberg had agreed to come along. He had been spending some time with some of the aspiring yachtmasters and was part of the team. His girlfriend Nancy came for the sail too.

We were to sail 24 hours every day for a week, sleeping in our wet clothes, using a shift system on watch: four hours on, four hours off. When your three-man watch was due on deck, you would first make hot drinks for everyone, maybe a snack depending upon the time of day, then replace those exhausted after their shift. It was cold, so each layer in turn would go on: thick woollen socks, normal trousers or long johns, a base layer, mid layer, then the waterproofs, hat, gloves, head torch, and finally lifejacket and safety line. A boat of Michelin men. In turn you would spend one hour on the helm, looking between a spot on the horizon and the compass, trying to keep on course. The boat would roll up and down the waves, the newer of us trying to correct the direction with adjustments and then being told just to keep steady. You'd spend an hour as the number two, keeping a 360-degree awareness, looking for any black worrying shapes or mysterious lights, and passing that to the knowledgeable ones. Finally you would step down below and spend a thankful hour working on the chart, keeping aware of the electronic device that beeped and showed everyone out on the water.

Freezing waves crashed relentlessly around and over us and winter wind drove into our faces. We were unable to stand up, having to clip on to safety lines before we could even get on deck. We shared our own treats, helped each other put lifejackets on, went back to our military training, back to a buddy-buddy system.

We, the veterans, loved every minute of it.

'I'd like the foresail up please, Dan,' Fish requested.

Fish had a calm demeanour about him. Everyone loved sailing with him as he always seemed at ease. He never shouted, only ever raising his voice to be heard over the wind. Dan, as first mate, passed the request down to the deckhands.

The prevailing southwesterly winds had built the swell and large waves were hitting the boat beam-on, accentuating the roll. Not good for everyone's stomachs but great to sail. Raising the foresail needs three people on the starboard lines, three people on the port lines, one person to control the vang, one to look after the mainsail, and someone, in this case Dan, to step back, oversee and offer advice. There was always a run-through first so everyone knew the drill.

'So the first thing we will do is take the sail ties off. They get tied safely on to the doghouse. Then we lift the gaff up, one team on the throat, one on the peak, keeping the gaff level so there's not weight pushing into throat and causing a brake. I'll give you direction. I need a member from each team to call back and let me know what's going on. All good?' he explained.

Everyone nodded and took up their nominated posts. Dan gave the nod to the Fish that all was ready.

'Helm to wind,' Fish asked.

I turned the helm as asked and felt the wind move from behind my right ear, across my face until it was full into my eyes. With such a big beast the timing is crucial, slowing the turn way before to stop the motion in the right place, until the Turk's head knot on the wheel ran through my hands and I knew the boat and rudder were all pointing in the right direction.

I nodded to Fish.

'Hoist sail,' he said. The message passed to Dan and the action started.

As with all manual labour, timing and technique is key. One person 'sweats', pulling on the line and driving the slack they've gained towards the pin that the line wraps around, the other then 'tails', pulling the slack gained by the other so that the next pull makes more gain rather than going nowhere. Everyone had been trained, but people warm to new techniques at different speeds. The sail slowly made its way up, seesawing until it became taut and the wind licked along the inside and outside of the sail.

'060 degrees, please, helm,' instructed Fish after getting the OK that the sail was fully up.

I turned the helm, waiting for the wind to take hold, pushing one way while the keel below pushed in the other direction, generating force and motion.

'060,' I told Fish.

'Trim to course please.'

Now Dan would look at the sail, judging to see if it was giving maximum propulsion, and by either tightening or loosening the mainsail, make sure the topping lift or vang was at the right tautness to see if that little extra could be got.

'What's the horrible noise?' Fish asked his now-famous rhetorical question and turned a tiny innocuous key on the doghouse. The engine stopped.

Smiles ran all the way up and back along the deck, heads nodded. It truly is a wonderful feeling having nature drive such a beast of a boat. There is something primal about it, a window to the past.

We were set. Fish went down to the doghouse to check the charts and start the log, letting Dan know he was now in charge on deck.

Dan wandered up to me.

'Mate, you want to sort the deck out, I'll have a go on the helm.'

'Roger, bud, I'll get someone on the brews as well.'

'Wets, you mean,' he corrected.

'Whatever, the fucking hot beverages,' I replied.

'Well, we are the senior service,' Rich chimed in.

In the army hot drinks are called brews, in the navy and marines they say wets. The RAF only drink champagne in five-star hotels so they don't count. This difference is small, yet significant.

After the deck was tidied and everyone settled into routine, people became a little more aware of their feelings, in particular, their stomach.

Two simple but wonderful cures for seasickness are, first, being on the helm, and second, being busy. Being on the helm makes you concentrate on a larger picture, including the horizon. Being busy means your mind is not listening to your stomach, which is otherwise being told to be angry by your inner ear, the confusion arising from the inconsistency between what the eyes see and what the body feels.

Nancy appeared from below with a plate of cocktail sticks on which were olives wrapped in a skin of bacon, a little pick-me-up while she prepared something else to wow the troops. Pete, being no doubt used to this high level of maritime cuisine, took one. Some of the others, coming to terms with how fairly the gods where smiling over us, also tucked in, then started emptying their guts over the side again.

At sea, when the sun sets, it's magical, whatever time of year. The sun had set right behind. Once we were out of Falmouth and south enough to pass Gammon Head, the promontory headland by Salcombe, it was a clear run all the way to the English Channel, so, dependent on traffic, the course had been pretty much due east.

On deck were three people. They were taking turns having an hour on the helm, then rotating inside to sit in the doghouse so as not to get too cold, making roll-ups for those outside and keeping the drinks coming.

Below deck, the radio spluttered into life.

'This is the Met Office weather forecast issued at 0800 UTC on Tuesday 5th January 2016, covering the period 0800 UTC Tuesday 12th January to 0800 UTC Wednesday 13th January 2016.'

Maritime forecasts are generally pretty much on the button. This one made everyone take notice.

'Wind west veering southwest, 7 to severe gale 9, perhaps storm 10 later. Sea state high or very high. Weather squally showers. Visibility poor.'

To many those were just words. To a few it meant a difficult period ahead. To an even smaller group, it spelt potential disaster. A force 9 meant 7- to 10-metre waves and a wind speed of 50mph. If it did increase to a force 10 it became even more treacherous. The Beaufort, the international method of scaling maritime weather, has a section describing what land conditions would be like for a force 10 and it reads: 'Trees are broken off or uprooted, structural damage likely.'

That said, *Spirit* was a big boat. She could handle tough conditions, some might say she preferred them. And so the decision was taken to carry on.

The sail plan consisted of a foresail and staysail goose-winged. The wind was right up our chuff, pushing along at quite a pace. As long as the wind direction remained the same, even though it was tough to keep on course, all would be fine.

People started to go down. Ian, an infantry officer who had spent time in Iraq and Afghanistan, had spent the last 24 hours lying on the saloon benches, suffering severe seasickness. Stevie, an RAF officer, had been bedridden for the last two days, only able to surface every now and then. Even Bob the engineer had thrown up countless times.

I went on deck with Chris. I'd been struggling and had taken advice to get on the helm to stop the horrid gut-wrenching I'd suffered since leaving Falmouth. Chris had already thrown up so he was feeling better. I started to feel cold. The rain was driving from behind, my oilies were leaking and the dampness was drawing the warmth from my body.

Every soldier, whatever branch of the services they served in, will at some time or another have gone through the breaking-down and building-up process. It is character-building, apparently, which is hard to appreciate when you are lying in an ice-cold puddle for a few hours waiting for God-knows-what. Anyway, you tend to know when it's a good idea to change your clothing.

'Mate, I'm just going to go and get another layer, I'm shivering. Take the helm for a mo.'

'No worries, bud,' Chris replied.

We swapped some info on bearing and direction, then I stepped down into the doghouse, turning back to unclip my safety line. There were a few nodding heads in the doghouse. I gingerly stepped over them, holding on to anything to stop me falling, including heads and arms.

I began to think this wasn't a good idea but I was committed now. I slid down the short stairs to the galley and took a deep breath as an attempt to recover my composure to fight against the sickness. My nose got a huge, unwelcome whiff of the Spanish stew that Nancy had been cooking. I rushed through the saloon, pushing past poor Ian's legs. I had another viewpoint on his plight now, ripping at my jacket, trying to get air to my skin.

My bunk was close. I grabbed my jacket and turned, sickness in my throat. Someone came out of the heads. I bundled them out of the way, trying to mouth 'sorry' at the same time.

Back to the stairs, up, past the bodies. I can't do the clip, I need to . . .

I held on and threw up, a deep, siren-sounding puking.

Chris clipped me on as I knelt all pathetic in the gunwales. All I could do was nod.

A huge wave hit the bow and soaked me. It was both horrific and wonderful.

'He's a useless shite that boy. Feed him to the pigs, Errol,' said Chris, quoting the movie *Snatch*.

I was lucky. Once I'd chucked up I was fine; others were not so lucky. The crew numbers were getting thin for twenty-four-hour continuous sailing. Fish made a decision, bounced it off Pete, and we turned to port to get a night's rest in so that everyone could recuperate.

Four sweet hours later *Spirit* sat anchored off, and eight sweeter hours later, the crew sat in the galley at 0600 eating bacon butties and ready to get back at it.

The rest of the trip was far more comfortable, and as the wildness of the sea turned into the majesty of the great Thames River, we turned into a boat of tourists, seeing London from the sea, which historically is the proper way to see it. It is a trading port, always has been, always will be. In the past it was ships tied up as far as the eye could see with goods arriving from the far reaches of the empire. Today the trade is held in tall glass buildings in Canary Wharf, but the general process is the same.

We all wanted to visit two things: the Thames Barrier, and the home of the famous British Navy, Greenwich.

We sailed through the barrier, just. As we went through, an eddy tried to pull us in. It is only when big solid objects get close that the reality of the vulnerability of floating on water becomes apparent. The barrier is a wonderful piece of engineering, with a modern beauty to it, and it gets used surprisingly often.

Greenwich was incredible. We sailed past all the great buildings, the painted hall, saw the newly refurbished *Cutty Sark*, the Royal Observatory on the hill. This is the home of everything nautical that is linked with Great Britain. It is even home to time, Greenwich Mean Time being 0 degrees longitude.

We reached the London Boat Show on time. Shaun and Tamsin stood at the quayside. They had been watching the progress on Marine GPS, nervously and with a certain amount of pride. We were haggard, tired, excited . . .

On the second day of the Boat Show two salty sea dogs came aboard. 'Hi, we are lighthouse keepers from Beachy Head. We had to come and see who the hell was sailing past us last week. Did you know that everyone else on the south coast was rushing to find a safe port from that awful weather?'

. . . add: and pleased with ourselves.

The Boat Show was a great few days, chatting to the public, scrounging equipment, cutting deals – and having a few beers.

For the return trip, there was some change of crew; some as planned, others not. Ian decided he was not up for another five days of sickness. Rich joined us for the return. Bob had been standing in for him for the journey up so the crew were relentless in comments such as:

'Bob would have fixed that in seconds.'

'Bob, such a helpful guy.'

Even when Rich started suffering conjunctivitis on the return, all he got was, 'Stop sloping, Rich. Bob would never have done that.'

With the London Boat Show out of the way, full focus now fell on the Round Britain challenge. The reality of what this trip around the UK would be started to unfold. We wouldn't be the first to do it, not by a long chalk, nor the last. We wouldn't be the youngest or the oldest. No doubt in a garden shed somewhere even now two blokes named Geoff and Bob are building a floating banana to make the trip in. But there were a set of factors that would make our trip unique: the veterans.

All those who'd registered interest up were now contacted with the question: we're ready to go – who is still up for the challenge?

Chris's Story

I was born in early 1970s in the north, in Lancaster, a town up on the border with Cumbria, but we moved to a small place called Austwick in the Yorkshire

Dales when I was quite young. I was one of five kids. I had three sisters and a brother and so we spent a lot of time on the Dales doing what kids do. I don't remember having a happy childhood, but I guess it was OK. My father was a butcher by trade and he had a shop and I guess one of us was expected to carry on the business, but I knew it wouldn't be me.

When I was fifteen I was really into riding. We were living in a bit of a horse-racing town, not too far from the Catterick Garrison, funnily enough. I used to ride out for a trainer called Harry Walton, who was quite a big deal at the time. Then I started to fill out and I knew I'd end up too big to be a jockey. I was drinking by then. The fact I was filling out was working in my favour as it meant I could get into pubs and get served.

One night I was out in town and saw this guy who had been bullying me for a while. I thought it was time to repay him. We had a fight and I beat him up pretty bad. The police were involved and my dad got to hear about it. In those days you ended up in court pretty quickly. The judge said:

'Mr Bartlett, you have two choices. You are either going down or joining the Army. What's it to be?'

'I'll join the Army,' I replied.

Four weeks later I was away. I wasn't getting on with the family and I went down to Sutton Coldfield in the Midlands for my three-day selection. I first tried for the Parachute Regiment. Yanto will laugh at this. I was pretty fit at the time as I was doing fell running and I ran the 1.5 mile in only 7.23 minutes but I didn't manage to complete the push-ups. I did one less than they needed. So they suggested the 1st Battalion of Green Howards,19th Regiment of Foot. They were based only 20 miles from home so off I went for 36 weeks to complete my basic training: phase one and two.

In those days if you put a foot wrong you got a good shoe in [got beaten up] so you never did it again. After completing my training I was sent to Almer Barracks to join my battalion.

I remember my first day. I had shown my new ID card to the gate, had my kit bag over my shoulder and wandered into the barracks with my hands in my pockets. I hadn't gone but a few feet before I heard:

'Get your fucking hands out of your pockets on my parade square!'

I had just met the RSM [Regimental Sergeant Major]. What a wake-up call.

This was at the back end of 1989, so it wasn't too long before most of the Army was getting into the swing of training for the Gulf War. In the meantime we, 'A' Company, got sent to the Falkland Islands for six months. The weather in the Falklands is ridiculous. You would get four seasons in one day: sun, rain, sleet, snow. But we were training for desert warfare. We ran around everywhere with our full NBC [Nuclear, Biological, Chemical] kit on. It got a bit silly. We would be sitting in the cookhouse trying to eat sausages with this great big heavy kit on. But we were eager. At that time there was quite a drinking culture: it was work hard, play hard. You'd be out until 3am, then have to do a PFT [Personal Fitness Test of running one and a half miles in seven and a half minutes].

After that tour was over we got sent back to Almer Barracks. It became pretty obvious that we weren't going to be part of the Gulf effort as the task force had already been chosen. We got sent to Northern Island, Londonderry. It wasn't like it was in the 1970s but it was still a tough place. No one would talk to you. Whatever you did, everyone still hated you.

When we turned up I was shitting myself. It was the first time I'd been in what was effectively still a combat zone. Within 12 hours I was in a V8 Snatch doing patrols. I was covering forward when a huge rock was thrown by the locals and hit me square on the back of the head. It knocked me clean out and I collapsed on the floor. When they got back to camp, they opened up the back of the vehicle and I rolled out. A great start.

That was the first of what became six tours of Northern Ireland, two of which were eighteen months long. We had been reassigned to a new concept called the 24 Mobile Brigade. The idea was that we would be ready to be flown forward by helicopter anywhere in Europe where the enemy had punched a gap, and we would then plug the gap until the cavalry arrived. We didn't spend that much time on choppers though. We were always getting around by 'heli-bedford', the Army 8-tonner truck.

In 1995 we had just arrived in Germany when the colonel told us we had 72 hours to re-equip as we were going to Bosnia. I went as a vehicle commander and we spent seven months there in total. It was horrendous.

Our vehicle would leave the camp full of fuel, 3,000 rounds of link for the chain gun, 120 rounds for the 30mm, and within ninety minutes we'd be back at the camp out of ammo and handing over to the next guys to go out on their patrol. At night, during foot patrols, we would be tasked with shooting dogs. They were in huge angry packs and were eating the bodies of people who had been killed during the day. I guess I knew it was rough but when you have a job to do, you become cold to it. It's just another body, then another. It's only years later it becomes something.

The worst thing I saw was heavily pregnant women who had been strapped to lampposts and had their stomachs cut open. I still can't get my head around that. That was sick. We could always tell when a torture chamber was close as there was a heavy smell of pork, as they would use blowtorches on people's skin to make them talk. Shitty times, but you just got on with it.

Under the UN our hands were tied. When we became NATO the conflict was finished in six weeks.

It frustrates me now watching the news. We are just sitting back and letting it happen again. That's what we are seeing in Syria now. We are not learning from the past.

In 2005 we were sent to Pristina in Kosovo, another change of role. Now we were doing static covert surveillance, tasked to hunt out people causing atrocities even after the war had finished. Sitting in blacked-out vans, watching people, watching villages, then calling in support.

I originally got injured in 2002, on a Saxon Commanders course. It took place in *Last of the Summer Wine* country in the Yorkshire Dales. We had all been told we had passed and just had to get the vehicle back to the depot. I was keen and volunteered to drive her and the team back. As we were travelling back a hay lorry came down the hill in the opposite direction. It was going at quite a clip and it got the speed wobbles, no doubt because it was top heavy. It forced us off the road and we went tumbling down an embankment and hit a tree. My right hand got wedged in a latch and my fingers got smashed. I got cas-evaced, but it all ended OK.

The second time I got injured was in Afghanistan, near Musa Qala. We were driving along and some of a bank gave way and my vehicle rolled over, down an embankment. All the munitions boxes went everywhere and some seriously crushed my head. I felt OK at the time; it was only later I started blacking out. I went to the med centre to see what I could do. They said I had to attend the mess do as I was CSM [Company Sergeant Major], so I did. During the evening I collapsed and got cas-evaced to Cyprus. They flew my missus out to Cyprus because they didn't think I was going to make it. I spent ten days in that hospital and don't remember a thing about it. I was flown back to the UK, then transferred by ambulance to Birmingham Hospital. They did lots of tests and let me know I had a swelling on my brain. It was shortly after that I started getting mental health issues. I went to see a specialist and we decided together it was better if I was sectioned for my own health.

I spent another twenty weeks in a place in Basingstoke taking all types of drugs, then finally got sent home.

I sat in front of a medical board who decided that I was unfit for service due to both my head injury and my hands. I was gutted. Army life was all I had known and before the accident I was going for a commission as an officer.

Things weren't too good for a while but then I got involved with the charity Help for Heroes and spent time at their recovery centre, Tedworth House. One day I saw a leaflet on their activity wall about a charity called Turn to Starboard, who helped ex-servicemen by taking them sailing. I remembered that back when I was stationed in Germany I had been sailing a few times and had enjoyed it. I thought, what the hell? I rang them up and went down to Falmouth to complete my Day Skipper qualification. It took a week or two and I enjoyed it; lots of things I was used to. When I was finished, the owner Shaun asked me if I wanted to continue sailing and whether I would like to work towards my yachtmaster qualification.

'Take as long as you need, but we can get the ball rolling,' he said.

I realise now it's been one of the best things I've ever done. I'm back in a team, feeling useful. It's not medication, it's just doing it – as good a therapy as any drug.

There are lots of things that are like being in the Army but in a good way. Putting on your lifejacket is like putting on your armour before you go out. Checking that all your kit is in good order before you go on watch is like preparing to go on patrol.

When I heard about the chance of a Round Britain challenge I knew I wanted to do it, and I was so excited when I got the nod. I decided I wanted to do all of it, and that I wanted to do all of it on *Spirit*. It would give me lots of sea miles towards my yachtmaster qualification, let alone the experience of so much sailing and the challenge itself.

04

READINESS

'England expects every man will do his duty'
Lord Horatio Nelson

ALMOST TO THE PERSON everyone said yes, they
were up for the challenge, so now there was a new
problem. *Spirit* is only coded to carry eighteen people at a
time and now there were just under forty wanting to take
part. Shaun had his own boat, *September*, and after a bit of
checking to make sure it was legally OK, she went into the
mix. We just needed a visit from the yacht version of Santa
Claus: Mike. He had been in and around Turn to Starboard
for a while, his son had benefitted from the charity and he
had taken a few guys out on the Fastnet race a few months
before. His desire and ability to sail in whatever weather

had endeared him to all the veterans. Well, that and the fact he owned *Quivira II*, a 48-foot Rustler, the Rolls Royce of yachts, which meant that he was welcomed with open hands, feet, well, anything really.

We were no longer a single ship but a threesome, but *Spirit* would continue to be at the heart of the challenge.

With only a couple of weeks' break it was straight into the three sets of familiarisation training. Ellen, the office's resident Geordie, had, as usual, been nominated to organise the trips. She sent out Joining Instructions, of which the top line read:

'Please read all the information carefully.'

So woe betide anyone who turned up with the wrong equipment.

Another line read:

'Please pack whatever you have in a squishable bag, not a suitcase.'

That hadn't been in the joining instructions for the London Boat Show. One veteran had arrived with four hard suitcases and a pushbike. Never in the history of sailing have so many eyes rolled as much as that moment.

'You're not getting the gist of this sailing lark, are you?'

It was suggested that the offender should wear his cycling helmet for the whole journey, including in his bunk. All were satisfied by giving his expensive sexy bike a little kick when they went by.

Shaun was going to be skipper on the Round Britain, so he was also going to be skipper on these three tester trips.

Dan was going to be first mate; Chris and I had asked to be watch leaders.

A simple plan, three groups of people, three days each, getting everyone aware of what they had let themselves in for. Get the sails up and down a few times, get used to shifts, get used to cooking for everyone, learn general safety, become aware of what it's like to be in such a small environment. It was on these acclimatising trips that some realities started to surface.

The reason for the charity's existence is to help military veterans who have found readjustment to civilian life challenging. This is a huge remit. Everyone on that boat had one or more elements to their personal story that qualified them. Night times were the worst.

Shaun as the skipper had the captain's cabin. Above the saloon were two pilots' bunks that Dan and I had snaffled. It was noisy being above the saloon but we tended to overcome such challenges. Oh, and they were also the biggest bunks on the boat. In the fore compartment you had a bosun's cabin for Rich, a two-bunk cabin generally reserved for women, then twelve bunks in an open cabin.

Whatever issues people have, generally they will have found a way of dealing with them to enable them to make the best life they could. But at night, the demons come back and the stresses seep out: chattering, shouting, nocturnal Tourette's, the odd scream echoing out above the snoring. It was a jungle cacophony, but in this environment it was accepted.

'You were making a right racket last night,' said Yanto, an ex-Para who'd volunteered to be in charge of provisions, to one such person. 'Then again, you make more sense when you're asleep.'

Mornings we would sit around the table with our individual medication cocktails: the veteran's breakfast.

'Ooohhh, the blue ones really make me drool.'

'No wonder you're such a useless belter, they are for horses.'

During the day, people would need moments alone, a bit of time sitting right up at the prow 'watching out for lobster pots' but really just wanting a break, a small respite. This was fine, too, but it did add another level of complexity to an already stiff challenge.

Shaun was looking for his crew, the few that he would be able to depend upon throughout and who would be the 'staff' element of the trip. He had Tamsin, who would accompany us in the role of operations. There was Dan, who had proved his knowledge and had a natural love of sailing. Rich had been bosun for *Spirit* for a fair while so no one knew her better.

I wanted to have a role on the trip. I'd made this known and was waiting to see if I could continue what I was doing on the acclimatisation trip and take it on to the Round Britain challenge.

Shaun pulled me aside. Dan was with him.

'I want you to put the mainsail up. Have you done it before?'

'I have, yes, but it was a while ago.'

'Let's see what you remember then.'

One thing I did remember was that if you keep your hands in your pockets, it stops you from jumping in when there is any kind of issue and trying to deal with it yourself. It's better to keep out and instruct others in a clear calm voice. It makes you look like you know what you are doing. Even if you don't, everyone else in life is making it up as they go along, so why not you?

Anyway, the sail managed to get up in a controlled kind of chaos and everyone seemed happy enough. Always best to keep things in perspective: no one died.

Over the three trips, so many differing characters came and went, each bringing great spirit to *Spirit*. Each arm of the forces is a slightly different flavour of ice cream, but it's all still ice cream. The banter is what marks out an ex-forces person. The tongue-in-cheek in-fighting between each regiment is legendary. The Parachute Regiment call any cap badge that is not theirs a 'craphat', the Royal Marines call everyone 'pongos', everyone calls them 'bootneck', the Guards call everyone else 'chippy'. The Infantry are only able to eat crayons, the Logistics are a taxi service, the RAF are trolley dollies, it goes on and on. All part of the Encyclopaedia of Military Insults.

After all the taster trips, only one guy dropped out. He felt it would be too much physical exertion for him. It was such a sad thing to hear that someone who at one stage would have prided himself on his physical ability no longer had that strong sense of self.

'I just feel I'd let the lads down. I couldn't take it if I couldn't pull my weight,' he said.

He couldn't be coaxed, and with those few words he displayed great dignity.

On the trip to London *Spirit* hadn't been remotely tested, cutting through huge waves with ease and no doubt smirking as most of her crew were retching over the side. Her prowess was not surprising. She came from sturdy stock. We had a mission to get her safely back to a port that had contributed hugely to the story of Britain as a successful seafaring nation. It was decided we would travel anti-clockwise around the UK from Falmouth, leaving on the first of June and arriving in Liverpool in time for the party in late July, and having a great time visiting many other places on the way. On the whole trip there were to be ten of us veterans as permanent crew, plus three film crew, while another twenty-eight veterans would take turns joining and disembarking over specified four legs.

As the June departure date inched closer, the general tone of the office palpably changed. When an adventure is a long way off in the future, it is easy to agree to get involved. How many people have said they'll run the London marathon and then, as the winter training comes a-knocking, have started thinking of good excuses not to go, shrugging and saying: 'I would have loved to, but just now I have to go and do something else. I thought my old knee injury was fixed but . . . hey ho.'

None of this was discussed openly. For all the understanding and mutual support, no one was spilling their guts out. Going towards a challenge is a powerful thing. These were people who had at some time or another lost the trust in their strength and their inner monologue. This changes things, makes everything harder. Lots of emotions were sloshing around.

About a month before departure, the charity was to receive a very special visitor: Princess Anne. She had been President of the Royal Yacht Association, the governing body for sailing qualifications, for quite a while. It was an honour for a member of the royal family, and one who is genuinely interested in sailing, to pay a visit. Just a little makeover for *Spirit* was needed in preparation.

Anyone who has ever owned a boat or yacht will tell you that they are both a money pit and a time pit. The moment you finish painting something and turn away, clean the paintbrushes and plan to reward yourself with a pint, you glance back to see it somehow needs to be painted again. Luckily *Spirit* sends out good feelings and had acquired many a volunteer who would pop down of their own accord and help Rich with whatever tasks needed doing. Slowly the ropes got spliced and the fire buckets painted. There was still a while to go and she wouldn't be perfect but, anyway, maybe the royal family doesn't always want to have the smell of fresh paint up their noses.

All the crew members were invited for the royal visit. The staff, volunteers, trustees, board members, children and pets all turned up for a wonderful salute to what had been achieved so far and what was about to happen. Princess Anne went around and spoke to every single person. For someone who must meet thousands of people all the time she was utterly enthusiastic and didn't once give any impression this bored her.

We had a Monday night quiz team and were a bit rusty on royal family knowledge, so Bosun Rich asked if she would be prepared to come along and give us a hand. She accepted but said unfortunately she was due elsewhere. Shame. She gave certificates to two recently passed yachtmasters and that was that. Whether you are a royalist or someone who dislikes the royal family and wants to wander up Birdcage Walk with a pitchfork *à la* the French revolution, you cannot doubt how hard some members work, with nine hundred-odd engagements annually.

All that remained was to finish off the paintwork on *Spirit* using the colours that last year's chance visitor had inspired us towards. International Paints had provided the paint, Turn to Starboard was to do the work. Originally she was to come out of the water so the painting of the hull would have been quite easy. Sadly that plan fell through with the shipyard as the promises went from 'Direckly' to no one answering the phone.

Enter stage left our resident Jackson Pollocks. Two volunteers who shall forever remain nameless gave up huge amounts of their personal time and effort to splash paint all over the place, covering the tender with five or six colours, which if they had been as famous as the American painter would have increased the value of the boat enormously. While doing that, their creative juices needed further space, so they started to work on covering the pontoon, until it was decided a more traditional approach was needed, putting plastic sheeting down and the like. They shall never live it down.

Dan's Story

I was born in mighty Yorkshire, in Leeds. That is, me and my twin. My parents separated when I was eight years old, and my brother, sister and I went to live with Dad. In our teens we went to live with my mum and stepdad, who was ex-Army.

I come from a really big, loving family, lots of aunts, uncles and cousins. Gran was one of fourteen. It's one of those families where, when we get together for a family occasion, by the time you've said hello to everyone it's time to start saying goodbye. We spent a lot of time with my grandparents when we were kids. They lived in the flats where my mum and dad grew up, so we would all descend on them for sleepovers all the time. It would start off with one going, then before you knew it there would be a load of us there.

I went to the local school, where my mum and all my aunts had been. In 1985, when I was five, one of my cousins joined the Corps. It was then I decided that's what I wanted to do.

From then on it was nothing else for me but the Marines and joining the Corps. Neither my twin nor I were particularly academic, so at 16 he walked into the Army Careers Office and said he wanted to join up. He was put into the Artillery and went down to Pirbright to do his basic training. I remember going to see him pass out. I had signed up for the Marines by now but it was a far longer recruitment process to get in so I was a bit behind him.

While I was there a colonel walked up to me.

'Have you ever thought of joining the Army?'

'No, I'm joining the Marines,' I answered.

'Oh dear, well, we've lost one to that lot then.'

It was my first experience of the banter in the forces and being snubbed as a bootneck.

My brother ended up going the pink way and joining 7 Para. He showed me how to put a rifle sling on, saying, 'You need to know how to do this.'

Then, when I got my first rifle, I knew exactly what to do. It was a nice moment.

The banter between us was always good, especially at Christmas.

'Oi, cabbage head,' he would call me.

I'd reply, calling him a Plastic Para as he had sneaked in the back door to be a Para by doing the engineer course and not the normal one.

We'd give each other grief, 'brew' vs 'wets' and all that. When he came home on leave I noticed his table manners had changed. We never wore a jacket or hat at the table but he'd be sitting there with both on, saying he had to eat his scoff as quick as possible. I suppose he saw changes in me too.

We still call each other cabbage head and pusser [another slang for Marine] and still adore each other. He lives in the States and has a great life. Good luck to him.

In 2000 I went on my first tour, to Sierra Leone. We were on exercise in the Med, which put us in a position of ready to move when the ship went into action stations. We were on the new HMS *Galahad*. I was stationed at the stern, manning a GPMG [General Purpose Machine Gun] with an old boy. He told me he had been on the original HMS *Galahad* when it had been hit by the Argentinians in the Falklands.

'This is really weird, it feels just like when we went down south in 1982,' he said.

I guess I realised then that we were going into something real.

On the way down my CSM spoke to me. 'How do you feel?'

'This is why I joined up, sir,' I answered. It may sound flippant now, but it was exactly how I felt.

I ended up going there four times in total. They all blur into one, though, as they were quite short tours. We'd go in, do our job, then come out. It's our role. We'd been extracting people from hotels, doing over watch [overlooking from a good vantage point], getting the staff from the consulates out.

The RUF [the rebel army] had been going into villages, nabbing kids, getting them hooked on drugs, training them. Then they gave them machetes and sent them back to their own villages to attack their own families. They would get banished from the village and end up totally reliant on the RUF.

There were also the West Side Boys, a militia who were supposedly working with us, telling us where we could find RUF troop locations. But they would betray us all the time, trying to kidnap NATO forces as well as the local forces.

The Paras had already been deployed to secure the airport. There was always the banter with the Paras.

'Finally made it then,' they would say when we arrived.

'Just look after the airport, will you, while we go and do a real job,' we'd reply.

Things didn't affect me too much while I was there. You just get on with it. But now I have a daughter it's started to catch up with me. It's mostly the stuff that concerned kids. There would be hair on the floor, or blood on walls in the outlines of the people who had just been shot. Kids being boiled in a cauldron . . . It's so awful, I can't understand how someone could even think of that, let alone do it. If you saw that in a movie you'd think it was too far-fetched. Real life is worse.

But as I said, while I was there it didn't bother me. I really enjoyed being a bootneck. I loved all of it, getting cammed up and sitting in ditches playing soldiers.

In 2002 after Sierra Leone I went to Northern Ireland. My grandfather had been in Sinn Féin; it was two generations ago so had nothing to do with me, but it does mean I have Catholic Irish heritage, even if it was Eire, so I felt I had a bit of a connection. We'd be in a car, just two of us, 22 years old, a gun down my pants, driving around Belfast. I'd had all my Northern Ireland training, but then it finally felt real. You'd see from the murals on the walls who was friendly and who was not. You'd have to be hypervigilant all the time. We got chased a few times but changed cars and got away.

In 2003, on my birthday, I was sitting on the border waiting to go into Iraq. I had a tweenies cake sent out and we ate that in celebration. We were all ready to go. It was planned that we would go in first, but at the last minute they changed the plan, the Recce and Siggies troop would go in first. They would set up then we would go in to take out anti-aircraft.

Then two helos went down. One got hit and it collided with the other. All the guys were lost. It was hard to balance being relieved that you were still alive with the fact that you had lost lots of your mates. I guess it's survivor guilt.

We were babysitting the journalist Bill Healy and he made a report to camera about it right in front of all the lads, who had just lost their mates. We just wished he had taken a few moments to move away from earshot.

We spent the next few days dug in on the salt flats. Everyone got the shits, so we were all wandering around wearing our shemagh scarves as skirts. Normal Marine rig – we do like a skirt.

We got helied into an area where the Yanks were getting smashed. As we arrived we watched stretcher after stretcher go with injured on them. The CO went off for a briefing and when he came back he addressed us.

'OK, lads, I want you to empty your Bergens, take as much ammo and link as you can, with water and snacks. We will be out for between 12 and 24 hours. I want to take this opportunity to say it's been a pleasure to have served with you all. I don't think all of us are coming back.'

We all got ourselves sorted, getting our rig together, looking at each other, realising the seriousness of the situation. We went out and, whatever we were doing, it was working: we didn't have one casualty. Loads of the Iraqis surrendered to us. We were patrolling constantly, doing dawn raids, acting on information. Lots of times we were suspicious of what we had been told. You never knew if they were just acting on grudges.

We tried very hard to be respectful, especially to the women, making sure their heads were covered. It wasn't their fault, what was happening to them, and we knew that. I found the cultural differences hard. I know you shouldn't judge other cultures because their core beliefs are different, but the way women and girls were treated astonished me.

When I had landed there I had hurt my back. We were malnourished and carrying packs weighing up to 200lbs, and when I jumped off the helo I felt a simple jolt, a crack in my back. But in that place you just carry on with it. After we got back, I went to Norway and carried on, but I noticed my fitness was starting to suffer, something wasn't right.

I went to the MO, got the usual pain relief and was told to get on with it. But the problem continued, so I returned and this time they sent me for an MRI scan. The results came back and the surgeon called me in.

'I don't know how you're walking. You've got crushed discs, you've chipped one of your vertebrae and you have a crack in your hip.'

I had carried on for three years. The original injury hadn't healed right and I had lost hip rotation and that had affected everything. It's the culture of not complaining. If you do, you are considered weak.

I knew this would be an issue so I went on an armourer's course to ensure I could stay in the Marines but in a non-operational role. After I completed that I went up to the med board.

After ten minutes deliberating they came back to me.

'Sorry. You are a Royal Marine so you have to be operational, whatever your day job is, and therefore you are no longer required.'

I was numb. They showed me to another room where a woman helped me sign a few forms.

I said I'd just go back to camp to drop a few things off.

'I'm sorry, you're not allowed, that's you done,' she told me.

I took my uniform off, put it in a plastic bag and drove home to Barnstable. I don't remember a single thing about driving home. I went back for my testimonial, a handshake, well done. It was over in ten minutes. That was the last time I was in uniform. It was 2007.

I was now left in the big wild world of fuck knows. I had no idea how to survive life, dentists, bills etc. I thought I went downhill slowly, but if you asked my wife, I'm sure she would say it was far quicker. Luckily I landed a job in a rehab clinic. It only paid 9K a year but it was enough to put a roof over our heads. I hid my own issues by dealing with others'. I worked all the time, until I burnt out and started drinking too much. I went back to Leeds to live with Mum to try and sort myself out. I had split up with my wife and got jobs with mates, working on building sites, hiding it all by partying.

I ended up in Combat Stress, doing their PTSD programme. I think I still struggle to deal with how all that affected me, how I became an arsehole, not being there as a dad and husband. At times I could see the way my wife looked at me, thinking about what could have been. She's happy now though, and that's great. I know now that it was the kids that stopped me throwing myself off a bridge.

I went to a mate's party. His missus worked for a Marines charity and she asked me what I was going to do now. I didn't have an answer. But she knew of a charity that was working with veterans and she knew I liked sailing. By now I had worked a bit with The Prince's Trust, so she suggested becoming a sailing instructor. She found Turn to Starboard for me, so I went there, but it was hard. I sat in the carpark for ages, so fearful. I took the keys out of the ignition to make a statement to myself that I was staying and not running away, which is what I really wanted to do. For some reason I made a pact with myself. No one knows me here, no one will prejudge me. If I get out I can be the Dan I used to be, how I want people to know me.

I went and met the team. There were loads of old bootnecks in the office and they made me feel really welcome. I stayed a fortnight, then went home and got some stuff and came straight back. I didn't leave for seven months, volunteering for that time. I enrolled on their Zero to Hero programme and now I'm an instructor. I still have my demons, but now I fight them. It's OK to not be OK here. Giving back to others has made the world of difference for me.

05

FALMOUTH TO THE ISLE OF WIGHT

'We must not forget to sing in the lifeboats'
Enlightenment historian Peter Gay
writing about Voltaire's Candide
(often misattributed to Voltaire himself)

FALMOUTH, 1 JUNE 2016

ALL STOOD AROUND SMILING and watching Shaun speak, his voice breaking, moistness filling his eyes. He started to blubber. A few shouted, 'Speak up!' Then others added, 'Stand up!' as he wasn't the tallest in the room. He got on a chair and was now at most people's head height.

Today was the day: 1 June 2016 – 2,000 miles and two months to go. For many it was the start, but for Shaun and his family it had been a project in the making for months. He thanked his wife for her understanding and promised to spend more time with her on his return.

The room was full of family and friends. The participants all had their grey fleeces on, proudly displaying the trip's logo. The mayor said something; other well-wishers also stood up.

A look around the room would have easily ascertained that those wearing grey were not fully present, that their minds were elsewhere. A feeling of anticipation was quite tangible.

'I just want to get going now. I hate all this,' Chris whispered.

'Agreed, mate, but this isn't for us, is it?' I replied.

Some of these men and woman had been on five, six or even more tours of duty. That could mean a period of more than three years away from family. That is a sacrifice you don't hear too much about. Quite rightly, those who put themselves in harm's way for the benefit of others do receive respect, but the family don't get any medals – not unless their loved one doesn't come home. Wives, girlfriends, husbands, boyfriends, children – all were celebrating a positive process. They were continuing to show their love to their partner, to go away and heal and to come back a better person. A return, maybe, to better times.

Mark, our marketing guru, was in charge of the tracking software that everyone could use should they wish to. They could log on to the internet, click on a link and see a little blue dot showing the whereabouts of *Spirit*. He stood up and gave a short presentation to everyone on how to do this, then ended with the schoolboy error, 'Any questions?'

'Yeah, why do gorillas walk like this?'

'Yeah, what's next week's lottery numbers?'

Mark hadn't been in the forces . . .

Photos and interviews ensued, then that was it, 6pm, all to the boats and off to *Spirit*. She had been moved off the pontoon a little earlier as her berth means she rests on the bottom at certain times of the day. The newly christened tender the *Jackson Pollock* delivered all to their respective boats, *Spirit*, *September*, and *Quivira II*, and everyone got on with their duties. The anchor winch slowly pulled in the chain and, a few hundred metres away, the Falmouth Marine Band played their drums. People waved, shouted and made merry.

The saddest news was Rich. Rich wouldn't get to join us as bosun. He had spinal surgery five days before *Spirit* was due to sail. He had his bags packed, ready to go, hoping to be given the nod, but it just wasn't possible. He wasn't recovered enough. He was gutted, having spent so long getting *Spirit* ready. At least he was getting the chance to make his own life better by getting much of his mobility back. He had made the best of what his condition had limited him to but now, for all the wise words and common sense, we understood his deep disappointment and frustration. All felt for him, and let him know as much.

'What happened when they opened you up and found you actually didn't have a spine?'

'What a lazy beefer.'

This time the weather was kinder than the London Boat Show trip. Once out into a bit of sea room, up went the sails and, just before Black Rock, the buzzing of the accompanying motor boats died down as they started to peel back to port. That moment of smiles arrived as *Spirit*'s engine went off and the magic of nature cast its spell.

Sailing consists of periods of huge activity then rest. On a tall ship there are a few more lines, a few more things to pull and fasten than on a smaller, plastic yacht, but generally it's the same. No one wanted to be anything but busy and contributing to the cause.

The three vessels passed St Anthony's Head and got on to a comfortable starboard tack. Not a huge amount of wind was available, so sadly the iron sail went back on to pop us along. *Spirit* weighs 88 tonnes. That's a huge amount of displacement and the science behind how she miraculously floats and sails was a conundrum for most of us. The pressures that bear down on the sail through wind are counteracted by the keel, which prevents the ship from breaching by pushing in the opposite direction. It's like when you put pressure on two sides of a soap bar and it propels forward out of your hand.

On the London Boat Show trip there had been maximum and continual wind so *Spirit* had got to 12 knots, her top speed. She was now travelling at 6 knots, engine at 1800rpm, oil temp OK. Every 15 minutes there would be an engine check, just to make sure. First the replacement engineer Tony would do them, then the job would be passed around. The marine-converted tractor engine was a bit of a squeeze to get to, but everyone needed jobs and tasks to use up all the boundless energy.

Getting into routine would be one of the first things to do: split into watches, start the process of getting used to the shift system. But the sun was still gleaming and cameras were out, taking shots of the sea, each other, arms around shoulders, selfies. Lots of laughing and joking. The clove hitches that secure the lines to the shrouds must have been tied, untied, readjusted countless times. Another cup of tea? Well, OK then, why not? We went past the five-mile mark, then a murmur swooped around the boat.

The engine was making funny noises. Someone thought they'd seen a bit of smoke.

Clunk!

OK, a little exploratory work, then it was just a case of letting the engine cool, adding a little oil, and off we go again. *September* and *Quivira* circled around us like two predatory sharks, the crew throwing biscuits. Nothing could dampen spirits though. After a while, the engine cooled, but it wasn't so easy after all. It was a gearbox issue, all nasty noises and smells.

Spirit was sitting just southeast of the land. We had no wind and no engine. The situation, although currently safe, could and would deteriorate unless action was taken. Shaun, the skipper, called everyone together.

'Just to let you all know what's going on. There seems to be an issue with the gearbox. We have tried some remedies, but at present I'm not happy with proceeding with it in this condition. This is a great opportunity to demonstrate the kind of situations you aspiring yachtmasters can and will find yourself in. We have no wind, no engine and a tide that will ultimately turn and start to push us towards the land. As skipper my first and foremost concern is safety. I have one more remedy for the engine to try, and if that doesn't work then at 20.30 I will call the Coastguard and the lifeboat will come out from Falmouth and tow us back. When that is the case, I want all everyone in lifejackets on deck. Understood?'

'So that means we will be back in time for the pub?' Yanto asked.

There is always a silver lining.

Spirit did get towed back. Luckily it was dark when she snuck into port. Well, as much as you can sneak with a 2.5-million-pound RNLI lifeboat strapped to your side.

First they had thrown lines to us. We attached them to the bow farings, which are more than strong enough. If it had been a smaller yacht they would probably gone around the mast. Then, when just outside of port, they had untied, positioned themselves on the starboard side, retied with bow and stern lines, making sure that their propulsion and steering was behind ours, and escorted *Spirit* in. A chosen few, sworn to secrecy, were on the dock to catch the warps.

The pubs were already closed.

What had happened had soon become common knowledge and I guess the team felt a little embarrassed. On board were quite a few people who had knowledge of marine engines, but more who had none. Of more concern were those who had none but thought they had some. Initially it didn't cause any friction, but as the days went by and various experts poked their head in, people's frustration started to find a way to vent. In offices up and down the country, if honest, open opinion is offered, especially against the status quo, it's generally frowned upon. But in military circles an open forum is allowed and there is an 'amnesty' every week or so to clear the air. It's a great system. People can feel free to blurt out any criticism, be it constructive or just nonsense, and not be shouted down.

To pass the time while waiting for parts to arrive, a schedule of maintenance was prepared. Many jobs required manual labour, various sticky, smelly potions and lots of trips to collect supplies from Trago. Those who are from Cornwall or have visited will know Trago; it's a huge department store that stocks everything. More and more often around lunchtime or early afternoon, a crew member working on a task would pipe up.

'Right, I need to go to Trago to get a spanner/tape/bulb.'

He would probably get one or two volunteers to give him help on such an important task and that would be the end of that until a bit of singing about 10.30pm.

Enough time had been put into the schedule for a few setbacks, a few slip-ups; they were inevitable. No one imagined it could go perfectly. However, we did also have fixed appointments and a final goal. As the first appointment was with the major sponsor, it would be good to get going.

Word went around that the engines had been fixed and that we were leaving for a quick test run around the bay. We stowed everything. People had a skip in their step. There was lots of bluster about the place and that communal feeling of movement. Geordie Al, who was ex-household cavalry, those guys that have not only their own brass and boots to shine but the horse's as well, had cleaned all the brass so that it glowed brighter than it had for a fair few years. Hour upon hour he had been swirling his Brasso-covered fingers on the ship's bell and various brass adornments. Cabinets had been built, everything had a new lick of paint and even the fire buckets had been replaced. More importantly, of course, she had a working gearbox and engine. Time slipped away a bit so at 5.30pm, in a little drizzle, or mizzle in Cornish, *Spirit* slipped warps again, this time a little shinier and more pristine.

September and *Quivira* had gone ahead, taking a few of the other participants so they could get a decent sail. Yanto had gone forward on one of them but got off up the coast and rushed back to Falmouth. His challenge was to sail around the UK entirely on *Spirit*, so that was what he was going to do.

It hadn't been advertised too much outside of Falmouth what had happened to our first attempt at leaving, but friends and families were quite quick to pick up that the internet's blue dot hadn't moved. Many on board feigned ignorance on the subject. A few slightly embarrassed phone calls ended due to 'bad reception'. Getting going again was joyful.

All cheered as *Spirit* passed the previous best of only 6 knots. There was a bit of catch-up to do but it was possible. The trip had been broken down into legs, so all the waiting around had bitten deep into some people's time on board. For a little while it would be 24-hour sailing, breaking down into watches, spending four hours on, then getting sleep and food. It gave time for many of the mariners to get their sea legs.

Spirit hides much of her talent below. First, the doghouse, into which you descend backwards. This structure wouldn't have been there on the original boat; they would have sufficed with an old tarpaulin. The doghouse was home to the chart table, radio and all the navigational equipment. On each side were two benches where those who were waiting to go on deck or were hiding from the conditions could sit.

A few more steps down was the galley, with enough room for three people to stand: two getting in each other's way while a third person who knew what they were doing would work. The crockery and pans had catches and bungee cords to stop them rattling around if the sea started to whip up. A few times on the acclimatisation trips they hadn't been secured correctly and mayhem had ensued.

The galley is a poor place to be if you are feeling a little nauseous.

To the left a concertina door leads to the skipper's cabin. It's the size of a bathroom in a regular semi-detached, which is a luxury on a boat. Unfortunately its location wasn't advantageous. Every few hours throughout day and night the engine checks meant that someone made a massive racket just behind the skipper's head.

An opening to one side of the main mast and a walkway to the other led to the saloon, the social centre of sailing life. Here was the heart of the matter, where briefings were given, meetings and meals were had, amnesties took place, jokes were played and lessons were taught. It was the place to lie if your guts wanted to 'do an *Alien*' and leap out of your belly, but at the right time of day it was a calming place. On watches, you'd just grab a bowl and spoon out some of the food that had been prepared and left waiting. During those times, food was just fuel. It wasn't the same as sitting around with eighteen people, laughing and joking. Brotherhood and camaraderie is

Spirit of Falmouth, a 92ft gaff rigged schooner, waiting patiently at anchor while the crew say their final farewells to friends and family, before departing Falmouth harbour for the challenge ahead.

One of the many interviews organised for the crew by Annie and Ellen from the Turn to Starboard office. This one took place in Scotland before slipping anchor for the Orkneys. Here the author is sporting the mandatory crew beard.

One of the watch leaders, Chris, pulling the sails up by hand. There are no winches on *Spirit* at all. The process is called 'sweating' – and it's easy to understand how it got its name.

Shaun, the founder of Turn to Starboard and a calm skipper, surveying the skyline for anything to avoid on the long haul from Yarmouth to Newcastle.

Adrian, a lifelong landlubber who has seriously taken to sailing. Whatever it is, having a passion like sailing is key to the quality of life for ex-servicemen.

First mate Dan, full of life and loving his new role, either 'dabbing' or showing us the direction to the Pentland Firth.

The original concept of the RB2016 was to gain sea miles and sea experience. Each day, one of the crew would plan the passage to our destination. Here Chris goes over his plan under the watchful eye of Shaun.

Yanto and Tony high up in the rigging, getting a bird's eye view as we approached harbour. *Spirit* proudly flies the flags of our two major sponsors, International Paints and the Endeavour Fund.

Chris and Dan working on the engine. This was in Falmouth after our first engine issues. Who was to know how often the doghouse floor would come up?

Al and Dan cooking up something between them, as designated by Dan and his headwear. The crew were always aware that if you made a public mistake, you would be punished.

Yanto and Tony showing how 'sweating' and 'tailing' works. Yanto is using his body weight to pull the lines and this pushes the gains down towards the pin. Tony then takes in the slack and uses friction to hold the gains. This can be a very slick process, but for a fair few weeks till we got proficient it was exhausting.

After what seemed like a lifetime the new gearbox finally arrived from Norway, and was gratefully received by some of the crew: Dan, Shaun, the author, Yanto and Spearos.

Yanto, the ship's resident ex-para, having sailed and flown around the UK, now has plans to drive around it in 2018. Yanto going up the rigging was a way of getting some peace and quiet... for the rest of the crew.

Clive, 'the padre', avoiding any hard work by hiding behind the doghouse whilst steering *Spirit* in the Shetlands.

The author being told, a few miles off the Isle of Wight, that we need to call the RNLI for the second time – caught beautifully on camera feeling like the gods of sailing are against us.

'Don't worry, guys, there is more chance of a whale landing on the deck than getting struck by lightning,' they said... a few minutes before lightning struck the mast.

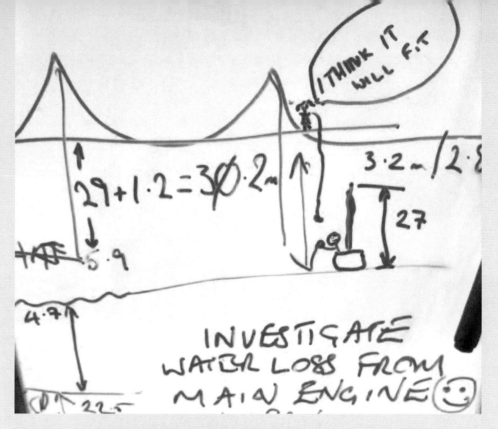

The famous algebraic calculation to avoid calamity. With *Spirit* passing under bridges there always needed to be careful consideration, as masts are expensive. Yet you never do know all is well until the moment you pass safely under.

For an island packed full of people there are countless remote places. Here *Spirit* is gently cruising past Oransay in the south west of Scotland.

Every now and then when time allowed, the rods would come out and a few fish would be caught to expand our supplies, unless the seagulls pinched the catch.

Navigating at night can sometimes be easier. Lights are coded so that they flash at certain times and colours differ from those around them. But when a light isn't on the chart it causes confusion. This is the light that drove the author and Dan to distraction entering Wick, Scotland.

Al and Dan are pulling up the sail from the starboard side whilst the author and Tony pull it up from the port side. You have to keep in time otherwise the sail raises out of kilter and can wedge itself against the mast. Something you learn to master.

Spirit arriving into Newcastle after a long slog of 400 miles from the Isle of Wight, with constant 24 hour watches along the way. We had missed a few dates but still received a wonderful welcome at the dock.

Safely arrived at Wick and waiting for the frightening prospect of the Pentland Firth, one of the most dangerous tidal flows in the world.

The Italian church in Orkney, built from bean cans and other simple materials by Italian PoWs, a wonderful and stunning place in one of the far corners of our islands.

The infamous kangaroo court. At least once a week, court would be called and sentences passed for infractions, mostly resulting in childish humiliation for the victim.

Court jester Al, putting the Al in morale and sending some water bombs over to other crews. This happened a few times, sadly without a single direct hit.

Spirit heeling slightly under way. Being 92ft and built sturdily, she was easily able to deal with rough seas – better than the crew, sometimes.

The celebrations begin. There was relief at being home, but also a certain feeling of loss and wanting to go again.

After two months away from home, Shaun opens a well-deserved bottle of champagne on *Spirit*'s return.

The three yachts passing Black Rock in the outer harbour of Falmouth, like three Spitfires coming out of the sun.

How wonderful to be met by friends and family, local dignitaries and general well-wishers.

The media shot before we left: the full crew for the first leg, brimming with excitement and trepidation.

instilled into forces people so deeply that when it isn't there, they can wilt. Purposefulness gives relief, focus gives energy, but the feeling of being part of something bigger is a human need.

Above the seating in the saloon were the pilot bunks where Dan and I slept. Here you get the cooking smells first, and maybe coffee in bed if someone knows you're awake. You get to hear as many conversations as you like, or drift off into a headphone-assisted sleep if you don't. You also get the sounds of Velcro being unfastened by people coming off shift in the middle of the night. Some were quick and efficient at tearing in short, sharp bursts. Others were slower, making the sound linger. Bastards.

These bunks give about eight inches' headroom when you are prone, so it's best to pad the beam above your head until you get used to your surroundings, unless you have a concrete cranium. Another benefit of sleeping here is getting to descend from your bunk in the morning with just your underwear on and climbing over people eating a bacon sandwich. Oops! Sorry about that.

Dan and I had each invested in a thermal blanket as a comfy under-sheet and a duvet instead of a sleeping bag, but the most snug berth award didn't go to either of us. Through the bulkhead on the left was Tamsin's cabin, her quiet place of respite from her seventeen 'naughty uncles' (her own words to describe the crew).

Tamsin was single and would always remain single. Her thirty-five uncles on the three vessels had decided that early on. She had no need for a man, we were all quite enough, thank you. Many a time at a social event she would resemble a VIP being protected by a group of burly bodyguards, all scowling at her well-intentioned admirers. One conversation in the doghouse consisted of the minimum ten traits any suitor would have to display and the ten trials he would have to complete to win her hand.

Going further into the forepart of the ship is the general cabin space where most of the bunks were: aka 'the jungle'. Those on longer legs of the challenge made their bunks as homely as possible. Chris had kept a military theme: he had served in the Green Howards before they were amalgamated into the Rifles in June 2006 so had a regimental-branded privacy curtain, pillow and duvet. He won the snuggest bed award. Under all these bunks were compartments containing tools and other bits and bobs. During the course of the day, people would be in and out of them, asking permission to mess a person's bed space up, then returning it to its original condition. Unless it was Chris's. That you left in a state. Shouldn't have brought a regimental duvet, should he?

Right up in the bow was the chain locker. If for any reason the chain got caught, you'd be in there with a stick wiggling it free, getting covered in grease.

This wasn't the below decks that an old pilot from the original ship would have recognised. *Spirit* had been built as a training ship and so now had far more comfort than it had originally.

'Sorry, bud, I forgot to wake you, better get on deck, we've lost engines.'

I heard this but wasn't awake enough to register who was speaking. In the night the engine had failed and once again *Spirit* was under sail but in poor winds. Up went the staysail, the mainsail and the gib, but even with so much sail up, she wouldn't tack. The gentle wind was pushing into the mainsail, which on a gaff rigged schooner is the sternmost sail. The gib we had up was too small so she was wasn't playing. The plan was to turn, but instead she would drift, being pushed from the stern.

In her defence, trying to tack in 2 knots with an 88-tonne boat was a bit optimistic.

The solution was pulling the mainsail down and gibing instead. The wind picked up a little but that wasn't the only element that needed to be taken into consideration. The chart put us at southeast of Durston Head, by Swanage. The tidal streams had changed and unless the wind started to pick up, the tide would be the stronger of the two and would push us into the rocks there.

With only 140 nautical miles logged since leaving harbour, it looked like we were going to need a tug again.

Another briefing was called and it was explained what was happening. Some faces started to look as gloomy as the sea. Breakfast went on, cups of tea got consumed and Shaun got on the radio to the coastguard. We learned an Irish tug was close by. They might be able to assist and give *Spirit* a lift in for free.

The tug arrived. After the usual 'Will you take my lines?' conversation we straightened out that, no, they were not that charitable, and, no, we did not want to become their salvage. Meanwhile a small yacht decided to sail between us, its grey-haired skipper with drink in hand relaxing with his wife. It would have been so simple for him to adjust his heading and pass behind, but as he was under sail, he did have right of way. It's just that sometimes you don't have to be such a dick about it.

And so HM Coastguard got its second call from *Spirit* in two weeks requesting rescue by the RNLI. It was Chris who had made the distress call. He had been volunteering with a local version of the RNLI and he knew all the guys, so he checked with Shaun and the call went in. At least this time everyone on board knew exactly what to do and looked super slick as the RNLI arrived and went through the same process. Not sure if that's a skill to be too proud of.

The RNLI is a charity that has saved approximately 150,000 lives since 1824. They are intensively trained and do an incredible job. We had huge respect for them.

There was a story in the news at the time of two American sailors, Bob Weise and Steve Shapiro, on their boat *Nora*, who had been rescued nine times in seven months while trying to sail from Norway to the US. They managed to reach Cornwall before listening to good advice and finally selling the boat. The crew of *Spirit* were also starting to feel a bit sheepish. too.

Spirit moored up in Yarmouth on the Isle of Wight, a small town that looks across to the English mainland. This was to be a home of sorts for a little while. Up went the banners declaring the charity and the challenge, up went the flags of our sponsors plus a suitable pirate flag, and up went the doghouse floor to find what was wrong with the engine this time.

The crew sat around in a beer garden under a raffia roof that was more akin to a Caribbean beach bar than the Isle of Wight. At least our weather-beaten, tanned faces looked the part.

'Lads, I just wanna throw something out there. Someone was trying to help earlier and got their head torn off. I don't think that's right,' said one of the crew.

We were ten days behind schedule, moored up with a broken gearbox and no sight of a new one. We had been towed twice now into port by the wonderful RNLI and the whole project seemed doomed. For the next 30 minutes around the table, everyone took it in turn to lay out their concerns, criticisms and complaints. It's called 'purging'. It's a forces method of getting everything out in the open, dealing with it, then finally putting it to bed.

'Right, so we are all agreed. Nothing leaves this table,' Dan said in summary.

No one blamed anyone. There is a definite benefit to having been at some point in your life under fire. Not at the time, obviously, but afterwards, when you need to pull together to get stuff done. It should be a question on a job application. Have you ever had rather nasty types trying to kill you? If yes, please proceed to the next question.

11 June is the anniversary of Mount Longdon, the battle 3 Para fought in the Falklands War, a war that for some reason has now been downgraded to a conflict. Yanto, our resident permanently maroon-clad Para, nudged me.

'I might need a few tonight, mate,' he warned.

I just gave him a wink, tapped his back and replied, 'No worries, Pink Hat.'

We spent the next few hours sitting in a pub, chatting and telling each other war stories, me more on receive, Yan, quite rightly, more on send. During the evening he either called or got calls from countless friends who had also experienced those brutal times.

'That's the way we deal with it,' he said. 'Talking. Not all those bloody pills you lot have.'

I woke up the next day with the familiar fuzziness of a hangover, mixed with the rattling bang of wooden blocks on the deck. Ouch! Beer, cognac and rum is a terrible cocktail.

It transpired that Yan and I had been the last pair back to the boat, and because of the tide there was a six-foot drop from the quayside to the deck by that time. Somehow we had managed to get on board and not wake anyone up: a minor miracle. Later that day I went for a shower. As I peeled off my top I saw I had a graze all the way down the side of my body. Maybe it hadn't been the result of heavenly involvement that we got on board, just old-fashioned gravity and soft mushy skin. Oh, and my phone was wet and didn't work.

By this stage we had been adopted by the town. Every member of the crew who walked into any one of the four pubs in town could order 'The usual, please, barman,' and get served with a happy smile and an enquiry into everyone's wellbeing, and that of the gearbox.

As the jobs on *Spirit* started to become less key and more of an exercise in keeping people occupied, I thought it was a great opportunity to have a wander around the Isle of Wight. My first bimble was from Yarmouth to West Cowes. The coastal path here weaves between sandy coast and sunlight-dappled forests and is quite breathtaking, not in a Himalayan or Grand Canyon way, but in a cute, quintessentially click-your-heels, what-what, English way. The sun was out, no one else around; yep, I had made the right decision.

After about four miles the path meets back up with the road. I had packed quickly and lightly, and therefore badly. I was getting the thirst of a vampire so I went to the helpfully signposted 'village shop'. It was 3pm. The shop was open 10–1pm then 4–7pm; some kind of siesta was in force. After a glance of the map, I decided not to walk along a grass verge for the coming five miles and jumped on the next bus instead.

I got into Cowes and my plan was to 'basher up': as in finding a nice forest and building something that Ray Mears would give me at least a score of five for.

The World Cup was in full swing. I was the only person on board who liked football. Watching football with rugby-lovers is asking for abuse to be thrown at you. England were playing Wales so with a local hotel at thirty quid a night, I decided to indulge in a bit of guilty pleasure. I grabbed a room and watched the match, no longer playing at being Ray Mears.

Cowes is like a mini Falmouth. Everyone wears luxury sailing gear and the town has the same friendly welcome. This is pretty much where the British seaside holiday started. Victoria and Albert took their holidays here, falling for it so much that they built the beautiful Osborne House. Soon all the acolyte elite rushed down to do the 'new thing'. It is a unique English great house, and it reflects her so much. She certainly was, to my eyes at least, a great monarch, second only to Elizabeth I. She oversaw a Great Britain that pushed the boundaries in every way: science, technology, colonialism. The sun didn't set on the Empire and all that.

My next stop was Ryde, a short ferry and a bus ride away, and another innovative place for the English seaside tradition. I found a plaque that mentioned a man named Donald McGill, who had his shop raided in 1953 and 1,087 postcards confiscated by the police. This was the man who created the famous 'dirty' postcards bearing cartoons of pneumatic ladies, weedy men and euphemisms. He was the spiritual father of the *Carry On* films of the sixties and seventies.

Sandown the day after: a walk and a bus ride. I had clearly arrived during the annual island mobility scooter race. The place was absolutely rammed with them. At the age of forty-seven I was by far the youngest person in town. I felt like an anarchic outsider showing off by using my legs to get around. But I met some lovely people and pottered around enjoying the faded glamour of this town.

It was time to get back to *Spirit*. Tamsin had located a new gearbox in Norway. It was being sent to Kent and needed collecting.

Yanto's Story

I was born in Tidworth, Wiltshire, in the early 1960s. I have a sister who's older by twelve years. She left home when I was young to join the Army and my dad died when I was three, so mostly it was just me and my mum.

I don't have any memory of my dad but he had a huge impact on my life. He had been based at Bulford Barracks, so that was where home was. Mum worked as a nursing sister in the Army Medical Centre. I had a good childhood, went to the local school. I used to get the bus there and back at five years old; none of this wussy stuff like nowadays. The school had lots of kids from Army families. My dad and their dads had all worked together. My dad was a captain in the PT [Physical Training] Corps. We had been about to move to Aldershot when Dad went to referee a boxing match. He came home and said he didn't feel too well, went to bed and died in the night of a heart attack.

He served for forty years, from the age of 14 to 54. He had joined the Para airborne forces before going to the PT Corps. In 1940 he was one of the PTIs they chose to train the new airborne forces. He went to the SAS, then finally back to PT Corps. He was the actor Richard Todd's sergeant major. They got injured together in Palestine in 1946. I used to go and see Richard a lot; he would give me free tickets to plays he was in. We would just sit there and talk parachute regiment stories while the other actors looked at us in disbelief.

In 1970 we moved to Moreton-in-Marsh in the Cotswolds. Mum became a sister in the local hospital and I went to the junior school. My dad had been a mason and it was his wish that if anything happened to him I would go the Royal Masonic School for boys in Bushey, Hertfordshire, which I did from aged 11. It was really strict. If you spoke out of line you got a whack. You certainly learnt how to stand up for yourself. Then one year I went on summer holiday and when I came back I was told that the school was closing. Then I was sent to Bloxham near Banbury. On my first night I got pissed and climbed up the clock tower. My house master was down below watching while I was trying to change the hands on the clock. I was always causing trouble. My mother was a Senior Nursing Sister and she would get all these letters back from school telling her about all the trouble I was in. She was so disappointed and she gave me hell.

I guess I've always wanted to be a paratrooper. Some of my dad's mates were captured during the fall of Singapore. One had this huge belly. I would ask him, why have you got such a huge belly? He sat me down and explained the Japanese made him eat loads of rice, then poured water down his throat until his stomach expanded and tore. This would only have been about twenty-five years after the end of the Second World War. They also gave me a bit of parachute they had kept. It was about 5 foot square. I took it home, climbed on top of the garage and jumped off. The parachute got caught on the corner of the roof, twisted and wrapped around my neck. I nearly hanged myself doing my first parachute jump. My mother came out, hearing the commotion.

'Stupid boy, bloody idiot! I just can't leave you alone.'

I wanted to join at 16 but my mother had refused to sign the papers so I stayed at school and did A levels in History and Geology. She wanted me to be a doctor or a lawyer and use my education, but I always wanted to be a soldier. At 17 I went into the recruitment centre in Cheltenham and joined up. I went home and told her. She went purple and had a complete meltdown.

Before she died I got to talk to her about it. She said she never wanted me to join the Paras. I was surprised. I thought she would be proud of me for following my father. But she said she had seen it, being around my father, seen what they would do to me. She knew she would lose her son to the Paras.

I started training in 1980 and on passing out I joined 3 Para, going straight to Northern Ireland. Before we left I went to the barracks where they were based. It was Candahar Barracks in Tidworth, right next to the med centre where I was born.

I went to Oman, then Canada, then in April 1982 I was doing patrol company selection when it was cut short due to the Argentinian invasion of the Falklands. They had invaded on the second of April; we sailed on the ninth.

The Falklands was an experience I will never forget. On returning to the battalion life was quite mundane. Many left the Army but I stayed on. I started looking for something else to do. I joined the Red Devils, having done a HALO [High Altitude Low Opening] course. I had a great time with the team.

I decided to leave the Army in 1994 because of the way it was changing, I worked in security, then three years in the police before leaving and trying other jobs. Looking for something that would satisfy, I set up a delivery business, but eventually went back into the security industry after Iraq and Afghanistan. In 2009 I was injured in a military training accident and had my right leg amputated below the knee. Since then I have tried to take advantage of every opportunity that has come my way. Turn to Starboard was one, and sailing around Britain was a fantastic experience.

06

NEWCASTLE

'Thousands have lived without love, not one without water'
W.H. Auden, 'First Things First'

ALL SAILORS LOVE ONE SOUND more than almost any other: the moment when you get out of harbour and can turn off the engine, leaving you with the sound of wind in the sails and the waves licking along the bow. Utter bliss. How ironic, then, when on the night of the 21st all aboard cheered when the beast finally kicked into life.

The Isle of Wight had been testing. The enforced layoff had stopped forward motion towards a goal, had even brought our completion of the challenge into doubt. As always happens in this situation, adversity creates strong bonds and ties.

Chris and I drove to Kent to get the new gearbox. Tamsin, Dan and Tony worked on fitting it until 2.30am, and Shaun, Yanto and Al helped with passing spanners and making drinks through the night.

The crew had spent over a week in Yarmouth. Two people stood out as new friends: Darren and Emily from the King's Head. They made us all incredibly welcome and gave everyone a home from home.

Finally *Spirit* slipped her mooring and so, terribly behind schedule, we were off and about to negotiate one of the world's busiest waterways, the Solent.

The stretch of water between the mainland and the UK is infamous for its traffic. There is a concentration of sailing clubs on both the mainland and the island, there are passenger ferries carrying tourists and locals back and forth, and there are the commercial boats that sail in and out of Southampton, Portsmouth and Gosport. Right in the middle of this mix are the Solent forts.

Back in the day when Napoleon was the scourge of Europe and threatening invasion, a man named Captain Stewart designed forts to be positioned in the Solent to protect the waterways. The idea was: if the forces of that little Frenchman tried sneaking up on the British, there would be the forts as defence. Four were built. Spitbank Fort, St Helens, No Man's Land and Horse Sand Fort were completed in the nineteenth century. They were never used completely for their original task and, as we already know, Nelson sank the French fleet in 1805, effectively removing the French seaborne threat. They fell into rack and ruin until being bought up by luxury developers. Now you can get married on them, whisk away your loved one for a luxury massage or even rent a whole one.

Our goal was far simpler. Just don't hit them.

Sailing in the morning sun, giving the ferries their mandatory distance and watching the Isle of Wight go past on the starboard side was encouraging for everyone. Sailing again, making progress, having a destination and a plan to work to – it was wondrous. A wave of quiet confidence permeated the crew.

The plan was to sail non-stop to Newcastle, getting back into watches of four hours on, eight hours off, and just eat up the sea miles with blind persistence, one of a soldier's most effective weapons. No stopping for selfies at the White Cliffs of Dover, just 400 nautical miles and 75 hours in one stretch.

The names on the chart, Black Deep, North Falls Tail, Knock Deep, were familiar from the London trip earlier in the year. Getting the charts out again we could see some faint marks from the earlier journey. The weather was kinder in one way – no waves crashing over the bow – but in other ways crueller, with no wind to carry the crew back on schedule.

On the way, Geordie Al gave us some lessons in how to speak to the locals.

'Y'all rit like' means 'Hello'.

'Way aye, man' means 'Yes'.

'Ah, pet, gissa pie like' means, 'Can I have a Cornish pasty please?'

Not sure what putting 'like' at the end means. Maybe it's Facebook speak, a verbal thumbs-up sign.

During this period the UK had voted on Brexit. The crew chugged through the Channel, France to our starboard, knowing the next time *Spirit* would dock it would be on an island with an undetermined future. There have been a few times when this island has had a wariness about its future. One was a fair few years ago when that bearded chap Drake was in his pomp. Philip of Spain had decided to invade England. Spain was Catholic and England was Protestant, and overthrowing Elizabeth I was Philip's plan.

He built an armada with plans to sail and deliver a huge army of 55,000. Drake first tried to burn the armada with fire-ships, which was effective in dispersing the fleet. The Spanish ended up in the wrong place, suffered from an almighty storm and got chased all around the UK. Relations have happily improved in the last five hundred years. I'm not sure if the armada was in anyone's mind when voting for Brexit.

Almost to a man, those on board thought that leaving the European Union was a good idea. Each had their own reasons, be it immigration or a desire for more independence, but patriotism is not a scarce commodity in veterans. Those few who were more European-inclined and had voted Remain were quieter. Maybe they felt that the crew had enough to deal with without something else to cause a split. There was enough of that on land.

As we sailed through the channel it seemed weird that many metres below the hull, people were sitting on the Eurostar, excited about their trip to France.

As the miles passed, the accents on channel 16, the open channel, changed. The mockney, Jamie Oliver cheeky chappie of the estuary gave way to a more rural twang as *Spirit* motor-sailed up the east coast. One of the unusual places in the world was not too far off our starboard side, the principality of Sealand. It's an old World War Two Maunsell sea fort. After being a pirate radio station in the seventies, one Major Paddy Roy Bates successfully stormed it, like he had at the Battle of Monte Cassino many years before, and declared it a nation. Although it has never received official recognition it has issued currency and passports, and now it's even possible to buy lordships and various titles. Paddy died at 91 without ever getting the recognition he wanted for his water-based nation.

Lots of British seaside resorts clattered by: Clacton-on-Sea, Lowestoft, Great Yarmouth and Skegness. Some of these were originally potential stopping places. Some were just names we all knew, so would be a good indicator of how the journey was going when coming on deck and getting an update.

The accents got richer past Scarborough on to Whitby, a place where everyone had wanted to go. *Spirit* was too big to fit in the harbour so plans were made to ferry everyone in on the tender. Who, particularly while on a boat, wouldn't want to visit such a historic port? Captain Cook, the very the epitome of an adventurer, hailed from here. He started in the Merchant Navy as a young boy, then joined the Navy and got involved in a war, one that at that time we were having with the French. During that he showed quite a skill at surveying, mapping much of the St Lawrence River in Canada. He was noticed, given the captaincy of HMS *Endeavour*, and sent off to Tahiti in the South Seas to record the passage of Venus to help find a method of determining longitude. The passage of Venus system didn't work as well as hoped.

He then sailed on to New Zealand and Australia and, as was his way, mapped everything. On his second voyage he was tasked with finding Australia, even though he already had. On this trip he made mappings that were still in use during the twentieth century. He was given a third mission to find a northwest sea passage. The powers-that-be in the Royal Geographical Society were full of ideas. Sadly, he didn't find it. After a ruckus with the locals on Hawaii, they thought it better to kill him.

The other thing Whitby is famed for is Dracula. It was here that Bram Stoker's fictional creation came ashore in Britain to become the first vampire superstar, culminating in a festival every year when Goths wearing fangs descend upon the town.

But for us it wasn't to be. The lights of Whitby slowly went from bow to beam, beam to stern as she passed by.

It is commonly said that, in sailing terms, the eastern side of the UK is less interesting. To be fair, the west coast, where the Atlantic Ocean beats upon the shores, is far more dramatic, but here on the east is a shallow sea littered with wrecks from the sea battles of the world wars. Countless windfarms stand proud to the wind, monotonously turning, sending energy back to the mainland: the new, precious energy source, trying to take the place of the traditional North Sea oil. Maybe this coast wasn't as sexy or as beautiful as the south, but it was productive, hardworking and honest: just like the occupants of the North claim to be.

Middlesbrough, Hartlepool, then Sunderland went past while Geordie Al abused them all, impatient to get to his beloved Toon. He was buried in the charts for a time then surfaced with his pilotage and skippered *Spirit* in.

High on the hill on the Tynemouth (northern) side of the river is a proud statue of an ancient mariner. Vice Admiral Collingwood, the right-hand man of Nelson at Trafalgar, was a local lad. It was he who took command when Nelson died. Sometimes it seems that the whole island is obsessed with one sea battle.

Arriving in Newcastle was a huge morale booster. We were back on course, on time, and it was wonderful to be reunited with the other boats and crews. The three craft hadn't been together for weeks, and we were welcomed with hugs of relief like prodigal sons returning from an odyssey. The crew took a few days to reset, and to re-stock food and water. Yanto went off to see some local friends; Geordie Al got to spend some time with his family.

The city of Newcastle has a main river artery and a history that has seen many a tall ship pass by. Somehow *Spirit* disappeared into the background. She was used to standing out and being the mightiest ship in port. But not here. Newcastle is vibrant, it looks incredible, with alleyways and cobbled streets all mixed with shiny new hotels and museums. Its population has a wonderful sense of humour. Go there; I recommend it.

One of the parts of the trip that couldn't be planned was how the crew interacted with each other – such a large group of people in a small space. Just when you get a routine, a way of working, it all changes. People say goodbye, some move from one boat to another, the pecking order changes, the roles get altered. All friends, all great people, but somehow it wobbles. Yet this movable feast of challenges inspired us all: 'It is not the strongest who shall survive but those most adaptable to change.' (This is a famous quote misattributed to Darwin, when in fact it was Harvard Professor Leon Megginson who said it while making a speech about *Origin of the Species*.)

Leigh from the film company Stick and Rudder arrived with Russ and Clive, both veterans, both ready for the next leg. Leigh would later put together a great 20-minute film of the trip.

We spent a most pleasant day sailing the staff of the main sponsor International Paints up and down the Tyne:

climbing the rigging, teaching knot tying and how to raise and lower the sails. All the same processes that had just been done for real, but this time in the quiet surroundings and slow timings of a Sunday potter up and down the river.

One more sailing push, one more round of catching-up time, and all would be set for the rest of the journey. Shaun called the crew together to let everyone know what was ahead. Newcastle sits about 60 miles due south of the English–Scottish border at Berwick-upon-Tweed. The next leg was to take *Spirit* all the way to the far tip of eastern Scotland. It meant more continual sailing, more watches, but by now the crew hadn't really known much else. It had been a period of frustrating inactivity interspersed with intensive work. Shaun, calm as usual, went through what was expected and who had which roles. There was now a race on. At the tip of Scotland lies the Pentland Firth and travelling through that was treacherous, to say the least. There were only a few windows when it was safely navigable. That latest window was about to close so time was critical. *Spirit* needed to be there as soon as possible.

The break in Newcastle had allowed people to recharge and to get perspective and having new crew members invigorated everyone. As we passed Tynemouth on the port side, *Spirit* sat just outside the harbour to wait for the two other yachts. Back as a flotilla, our business now was north.

As you sail further north, daylight does bizarre things. In these latitudes at this time of year it can stay light for what seems like forever. Coming on to watch at 3am and seeing light in the sky is bizarre. No wonder the Jocks have such a reputation for drinking – they must always think it's time for another wee dram. Yet night navigation can also be one of the most challenging processes because distances are distorted, as are lights and sounds.

On board, both day and night, every hour a fix is put on the chart using the data supplied by GPS and cross-checked with visual compass readings. All the relevant details are listed: speed, direction, sea state, wind and tidal direction. If all the electronic wizardry fails, there is a workable solution for either continuing or going back the way you came, depending upon the conditions. On most modern boats there is also a wonderful Automatic Identification System (AIS) that plots every boat, ship, sea depth, and buoy. This shows everyone's speed, direction, even potential collisions. You can zoom in and see what's around you.

Sailing boats generally travel between 5 and 15 knots. Some obviously go faster, but things generally happen at a slower pace than on land; yet with manoeuvrability and the constant shift of nature, accidents do happen. Generally, they take place near land, where there's lots of that horrid hard rock stuff that rips into hulls or other vessels that aren't playing the game.

Like anything, some people take to navigation and love it, while for others it is a foreign language, their eyes glaze over and they disappear into their own safe space. Military types have at one level or another been involved in navigation during their careers so generally they are quite adept at it. Getting lost and cold a lot will sharpen your skills on that front.

After we sailed quite a period on a bearing of true north, Peterhead passed on the port side. We were moving from one pre-planned objective to another. Every time the chart showed that a marker had been reached, another one was planned, the bearing recalibrated and readjusted.

That is, until red light appeared on your bow, one which couldn't be found on the chart and which caused concern. With no data, you can't work out how close or far it is. For us this was more than a little worrying as it was slap bang where we needed to go, right on course to Wick. We began a process of elimination. Does it move? No. It's not a ship then, unless it's at anchor, even if it's not showing the correct night light to disclose this.

We checked through every available resource to see what it could be: on a chart, in the almanac. Nope, still no answer. Ah, maybe it's not on the sea, maybe it's on the land. Yes, sitting a fair few miles behind Wick is a radio mast. It's not mentioned in the port notes for approach, yet it's the best navigational aid there. Panic over. Dan and I had puzzled for hours over this red light on our bow. I went off watch just as we worked it out.

Wick is in the far northeast of our mainland just by John O'Groats. It was once a huge herring fishing port before the decline of that industry. Now it is a quaint town full of happy, chatty locals. It can't have been more than ten minutes after our arrival before people were bustling around the boat and giving us donations. Well done, Ellen, for getting us into the local paper.

If *Spirit* had landed here nine hundred years ago it would have been in a place owned by Norway. The whole of the east coast of the UK had been plundered by Norseman, or Vikings as they are colloquially known.

If *Spirit* had tried to moor here two hundred years ago there wouldn't have been a jot of space. It was during this period that Wick was a huge herring harbour and fishing port. The herring shoals had abandoned the west coast and come east and the little town of Wick grew. By the harbour is a photo of the same view but with boats covering it. You could walk from one side of the harbour to another without getting your feet wet, they used to say. But those days were long gone. Wick is a windy place, victim of weather and its location.

Robert Louis Stevenson wrote of the town: 'Certainly Wick in itself possesses no beauty, bare grey shores, grim grey houses, grim grey sea, not even the gleam of red tiles, not even the greenness of a tree.' All of which may be true, but on the plus side they distil a whisky named Old Pulteney, which has won countless awards and is revered as one of the finest single malts in the world. Also, here is the world's shortest street, Ebenezer Place. It's basically a front door with its own postcode on the end of a building. After twenty-four hours everyone in the town knew who we were. Each pub had been visited, often many times, and many an Old Pulteney had been drunk.

Wick is also the stop-off point before entering the Pentland Firth, where the huge force of the Atlantic tries to squeeze through a channel only a few miles wide, resulting in treacherous waters with tides of up to 17 knots. Only the night before the RNLI had been called out to rescue a boat, with another boat then having to rescue them due to the high waves. Remember poor old Steve Shapiro and Bob Weise, of the famous professional rescues? Well, Wick RNLI had been called out to help them too.

Spirit had received enough help from the RNLI. Of course, it was because of mechanical issues rather than sailing errors, but caution was to be taken in such challenging waters. So while the crew made merry with the locals, Shaun, Dan and Tamsin sat with the harbour master to discuss the next leg. What became gradually clearer was that there was a difference between what the almanac gave as good instruction and what the harbour master gave as advice. That put us in a quandary, but Shaun felt it was better to go with local knowledge.

Al's Story

I'm Ashington born and bred, up in the northeast. Spent my school days here and my first dream was to be an architect. But when I left school in 1990, there was a bit of a recession on and a lot of people I knew were going to Germany to get work. I had a change of heart and signed up for the Army.

My dad had been a cavalryman, my grandfather was a cavalryman in the Second World War, my great grandfather was a cavalryman in the First World War. It's definitely in our blood so for me to be a cavalryman was a natural progression.

I was lucky, I got my first choice, the Blues and Royals in the Household Cavalry, the senior regiment in the British Army. I started my training at Pirbright for the infantry stuff, then Poddington for the armoured tank stuff then to Windsor for the riding stuff. Then after all that I went 'uptown', which is what we call joining the regiment when you've finished your training.

I was sent to Bosnia in 1996. It was horrible but I guess it's what you expect. I became numb to it all, the squaddie thing to get your head down, screw the nut and crack on. Everything was hunky dory until 2001. I was on parade when a dog spooked my horse and it flicked me off. I landed on my head, fractured my neck and suffered traumatic brain injuries. When I woke up I didn't know who I was or where I was. I didn't know I was married and I didn't know my own name.

I'd damaged my hippocampus, the part of the brain that controls cognition. When I came out of hospital I spent a year in Headley Court doing rehabilitation. They told me I could never go back to my regiment; that I only had 10 per cent cognition and this was how I would be for the rest of my life. It's crap, and there's no improvement. It's like having lots of boxes full of memories and a big set of keys but they are all jumbled up. I've had to learn to read and write again. When I see new things they don't register as a memory. I can't deal with money and stuff. My only hope is external strategies, loads of alarms telling me what to do and when.

So I became a civvie and was given a care team. They told me I was unable to do lots of normal things because they were too dangerous. I never worked again and sat in my house for years not doing anything, not even knowing where I was half the time.

I was terrified of being taken advantage of. I didn't trust anyone. I got divorced, became a hermit and didn't see anyone for years.

Then four years ago I was put in touch with the County Durham activity day unit. They helped people with brain injuries. People like me. It was a start; I got my driving licence back. I could use a sat nav to get me where I wanted without having to remember the way.

By then I'd met another girl and got married. My new wife wanted to get a caravan. But I reasoned that a yacht is like a floating caravan, so I bought a little yacht. The care team were worried and wanted me to sell it until I could prove competency. I got in touch with all the RYA centres up and down the northeast coast but none of them could help me.

Then one instructor told me about a charity that was working with veterans, teaching ex-servicemen how to sail. He gave me the number and I called them. Tamsin answered and two days later I was booked on a competent crew course.

I put the address into my sat nav, came down and passed my course. I was chuffed to bits. I went back and showed the care team my certificate. It was the best thing I had done since the Army. I wanted to keep going with the training so I booked on to a day skipper course, which takes a bit longer. On the last Friday, during my test, I was told there was a place available on the Round Britain Challenge, the leg from Falmouth to Newcastle, and would I like to go? Ellen kindly washed my clothes ready for the trip and I jumped on.

I had no time awareness, but it didn't matter. From the moment leaving and seeing dolphins just outside the harbour, I loved it.

07

PENTLAND FIRTH

'One's back is vulnerable, unless one has a brother'

Ancient Viking saga

MOST OF THE CREW HAD picked up on the fact that crossing the Pentland Firth was a big deal but the full seriousness of it hadn't sunk in. After all, this is the UK and we don't have anything really scary here. Our mountains are no more than hills compared to the Alps or the Himalaya and you'd struggle to get injured by any of our wildlife. We no longer have bears or wolves, although the reports of cow tramplings have apparently increased recently.

Luckily the sailing contingent of the group did give the crossing the seriousness it deserved.

The main passage is only about three miles long but this small distance is what creates the huge amount of tidal power. The whole of the Atlantic is trying to rush through this small opening, hence tidal speeds of 16 knots or 30kph. The area is littered with overfalls and races, or whirlpools with ancient foreboding Norse names like Svalga, meaning 'the swallower'.

The almanac's solution was to sail about three miles off the coast then change direction. The local advice was to stick inland and use the power of the eddies while you creep up the coast. Then, just when the tide is turning, you can use the incoming tide to glide across. You have to keep your nerve aiming at a nominated rock, the Muckle, when it doesn't seem to make sense to do so. Timing is key. *Spirit* had to be in a certain place at exactly 0904 hours – it was that specific.

Slipping lines in the morning, we couldn't have been accompanied by better weather. The greens of the mainland contrasted with the blues of the sea, and streams of sunlight struck *Spirit* as she slowly sneaked up the coast, hopping from eddy to eddy, ready for the curtain call of 0904, with *Quivira* and *September* just behind tacking back and forth.

Spirit arrived at her mark just on time and started crossing with all hands on deck waiting as the clock ticked. Hold the course, hold, hold . . .

0903 . . . 0904, then as the slack changed, as if by magic the whole boat started drifting. It was working. Bravo for local knowledge.

But behind was trouble. A dark squall was threatening to turn this wondrous crossing into a rather wetter experience. The two yachts were chasing to keep ahead of it, like two surfers on the head of a wave. As the three boats crossed, the squall, thankfully, decided to stay over the mainland.

It was decided that *Spirit* would nip into a bay just over the other side and wait, have lunch, then the three boats could rendezvous and go on together. Once *Spirit* was anchored, teams split up to sort out the food and so on. Some of the team were below for an unusual amount of time while glorious sun was on offer on deck, that is, until the mast and silhouette of *Quivira* was sighted.

Chris, Russ, Al and Clive had prepared a welcoming committee for the other two. What had taken the time downstairs was filling 120 balloons with water. The catapult was slung between the two masts and tested. Lt Col Clive Hunt of the Royal Artillery took charge and a few balloons were launched to test range. The trap was set.

Quivira came closer and into range so we all leapt into action as quickly as a bunch of veterans can and started bombarding them, managing to hit every part of the water around them but not managing to hit them. They sneakily, and in quite an ungentlemanly fashion, produced their own catapult. They had the ability to defend themselves. It was then that everyone on board recognised that *Spirit* was a much bigger target: splosh! We had incoming.

The other yacht arrived and got the same welcome. When the water bombs ran out tomatoes appeared. A few landed on deck and the shout went out to bring up tomatoes from below. Two tins of peeled Italian toms appeared. Nope, not suitable. Finally everyone on *Spirit* attached the two fire hoses and gave the two boats a complete soaking.

Somehow, the feeling throughout the ship then changed. It was like everything up until this point was some kind of race against time and now were all free. The disappointments of the first few legs were behind us and slowly disappearing over the horizon. The potential for failure seemed to ebb away. We had reached the physical point of no return and this re-energised everyone.

A stupid water fight also tends to help morale.

The next harbour was Stromness on the Orkney mainland. To get there the flotilla had to sail through Scapa Flow. Scapa Flow is synonymous with British naval history, especially during the last two world wars, but it had also been a key position for years before that. Viking longboats would anchor here. 'The bay of the long isthmus' was mentioned in many of the Old Norse sagas, no doubt for resting up before some more tiresome raping and pillaging.

In the First World War, part of the British fleet was moved north to counter a potential attack from the German fleet. Scapa Flow was chosen as the location for the fleet, imperfect but the best harbour on offer. To defend from U-boat attacks, huge amounts of ships were purposely sunk in some of the passages and entrances. This was to prevent the enemy submarines from getting a line of sight of the British Fleet at anchor. One tried to get through and ended up being rammed and sunk by a trawler; another was detected by sonic listening devices, then mined.

It came to a head in 1916 in the Battle of Jutland. Part of the British fleet left from Scapa Flow, joined with other parts of the fleet and engaged the Germans in the seas between Norway and Germany. After the battle both sides claimed victory. The Germans had inflicted far more casualties in both ship and lives upon the British but the British had contained the German fleet and continued to rule the waves.

At the end of the war, the German fleet was taken to Scapa Flow. While the heads of state discussed what to do in France during the Treaty of Versailles, the German Rear Admiral Ludwig von Rueter decided he didn't want the fleet falling into British hands and so scuttled his boats. It had been planned for months: welding hatches open, throwing key tools overboard, placing explosives in strategic places. Even though the British managed to stop a few from sinking, the majority did go to the depths.

During the next few years many of the ships were raised and salvaged to be ready for the next world war. In 1939 a German submarine got through at high tide, fired two torpedoes and sank HMS *Royal Oak* with a loss of 833 souls, before escaping back the way it had come.

The Orkney Islands have a history as old as anywhere in the UK. Skara Brae is a Neolithic dwelling on the mainland dating from 3000BC. A UNESCO World Heritage Site, it is known as the Scottish Pompeii, although for dating and style it's a bit more Stonehenge. Of course, around 900AD those damn Vikings turned up and decided it was as good a place as any to call home. They stuck around until they gave the islands back as part of a dowry to James III of Scotland.

Stromness itself is a small fishing town with a population of only about two thousand. It had first grown in the seventeenth century when ships from the Hudson Bay Company started to use this way of approaching the UK rather than the English Channel. The channel at that time was deemed too dangerous to sail through because England was at war with France. Even after the wars had finished, Stromness remained a stop-off and its prosperity grew.

First came the golden years of whaling then, when they subsided, came a herring boom, when the town became quite a rowdy place to visit. From 1920 to 1947 it became a dry town, as did Wick, banning the sale of alcohol. Luckily that wasn't the case during *Spirit*'s visit.

Once we were safely moored, a few popped off for what would be one of many tours around whisky distilleries. For a boatful of veterans, two local stories stood out: that of Churchill's barriers, and the prisoners of war who built them. Yanto, Russ and a few others got the bus over to Lamb Holm to have a look.

After HMS *Royal Oak* had been sunk in Scapa Flow, Winston Churchill, who at the time was First Lord of the

Admiralty, ordered barriers to be built between the small islands of Glimps Holm and Lamb Holm, between the mainland and Lamb Holm, and between two other islands. To build them they used a system that every soldier who has served in Iraq or Afghanistan knows. It is a metal mesh or 'gabion' filled with rocks. While in the desert wars of Iraq and Afghanistan these barriers were used above ground to build fortifications for troops, here they were sunk into the sea to stop those bothersome torpedoes. It was a huge undertaking. At the time lots of Italian soldiers who had been captured in North Africa had been relocated to Orkney, and they provided the manpower to build them. Now the barriers are used as the main roads between the islands.

Luckily these hard-working POWs left another memento of their visit. As Catholics they wanted a place to worship, so they sought permission to build a church. To say the place is remarkable is a huge understatement. They constructed a wonderful church from two Nissan huts joined together, with corned beef tins hammered to make candle holders and a car exhaust fashioned beautifully to be the stand for a font. The rest was made from cement. Hard work and creativity resulted in a permanent sanctuary in this most windy of places.

The man who decorated most of the chapel remained after the war to finish it, a certain Sr Domenico Chiocchetti. If you are going to be incarcerated as a prisoner of war, building a church is a damn fine thing to do with your time.

Everyone reconvened back at *Spirit* after the various trips for what was now a regular evening forum for sharing stories while breaking bread. It was now a whole month since *Spirit*, *Quivira* and *September* had left Falmouth. All were now sitting safely in the furthest point the ships would be from home. Every mile travelled from now on would be a mile closer to Falmouth.

Tamsin had had to find a way of getting her own space, being not only the lone girl for much of trip, but also a civilian suffering the silliness that tends to be the modus operandi of grown men brought up in the forces. Her way of finding solace was to don her running shoes and take a run around the hills looking down on the docks and ports that *Spirit* visited. Many a time she would return red-faced and rejuvenated.

After her run in the Orkneys she said, 'Watching the sun come up, looking down on the boat and seeing the crew getting up was magic.'

This was a trip of individuals but it was far more a trip of a team.

The plan was to visit Ullapool over on the mainland, but while we were pulling back out of the harbour at Stromness a funny noise started up. It cannot be underestimated how general high confidence can dampen awareness; how being full of good morale can prevent you from hearing things you don't want to hear. Shaun got on to the other boats.

'Guys, we have lost a bit of drive from the engine and will be monitoring it. Just letting you know so you don't disappear too quickly because we may be going back in to check it out.'

Within what seemed like 30 seconds there was a call for *Spirit* on the radio.

'Stromness Coastguard here, you guys need any help?'

Shaun politely declined. *Spirit* turned round to make her way back in. Then another offer of help came from a nearby passenger ferry, willing to change course to come to assist. Again the offer was appreciated but declined. Then a dive ship offered help and kindly tucked in behind us, just in case.

In a display of good seamanship, Shaun and Dan sailed on to the pontoon, using a bit of sail scandalising to lose power just when needed.

It is a huge testament to the people of Orkney how willing they were to offer help, and maybe also a reminder of how treacherous these waters can be and how many of these people had lost loved ones. It was 7am on a Sunday morning but word had already got around town and a few locals were on the pontoon ready to take lines. Tamsin got on to her magic ship-fixing phone and an engineer arrived. Tony sat with him trying to explain what had gone wrong.

'I dinnae care what went wrong. I just need to know what yer want,' he said in true get-to-the-point Orkney style.

During the time it took for a couple of the guys to nip to the shops to get a few luxuries during this unplanned pit-stop, the engineer went off, fashioned a bespoke part and fitted it, all for a pittance. Another day was spent in the Stromness pubs, some of the locals a little put out when Dan used Yanto's metal leg as an ashtray while standing outside the pub having a smoke.

Next day, as we were leaving for the second time, the wonderful landlady brought down a bottle of whisky.

'You can drink this when you get to Falmouth,' she said.

Back at sea going west, all were on deck waiting to see one of the most famous sights in this part of the world, the Old Man of Hoy, the sea stack just off the island of the same name. The weather was getting a bit changeable and the clag was arriving so it looked like it was going to be a no-show, but just at the right moment the fog and mists cleared and there he was. Another box ticked.

It had been decided to go straight to Stornoway on the Isle of Lewis and miss the planned stop in Ullapool because of having lost a day in Stromness. It was another overnighter. Early in the morning we got ready to pull into Stornoway harbour. Dan got on the radio to the harbour master to request a berthing.

'Aye, we've got room for you, just pull in front of the cat,' he told him.

Dan sent the message to the lookouts to watch out for a catamaran, and that we were going to be berthing just in front of her.

As *Spirit* got closer and closer to the beautiful natural harbour, the town became clear, but no catamaran.

Dan got back on the radio for more information and assistance.

'No, it's a fishing vessel called *The Cat*,' he explained.

Mystery solved, the size of the challenge then revealed itself. The gap ahead of the feline-named fishing vessel was *Spirit*-sized – just. *Spirit* is 92 feet, but 20 feet of that is a bowsprit that juts out considerably. Whereas in a normal yacht you can just aim the bow into the space and then pull hard to port or starboard at the last minute and slip nicely in, the proposed berthing was against quite a high wall. Oh, and obviously there are no bow thrusters to allow you to glide around sideways.

Lookouts were posted everywhere and in she went, bow first. Under the bowsprit is a chain that runs from the actual bow of the ship to the tip of the spit. It counter-balances the upwards pull made on the front of the spit from the front stay, which runs down from the foremast. The chain was just scraping over the top of the wall as 'Hard to starboard!' was shouted and *Spirit* squeezed into the space. Still three feet to spare – what was all the fuss about? Nice drills, Dan.

Stornoway is the capital of the Isle of Lewis and another place that got started by those damn Norsemen. Its ownership got batted around until in 1844 a chap called Sir James Matheson bought the whole island for half a million pounds. He had made his money from one of the British Empire's less honourable industries: the opium trade with China. He set about building Stornoway Castle, a stunning Victorian building looking down on to the harbour.

Some of the guys went off to visit, including Tony and Al, a natural recipe for disaster with Tony enjoying making up stories and Al's cognition issues.

'I wonder who lived there?' Al asked.

'I know,' said Tony. 'That's the home of the first keyboard player for Pink Floyd. He made all his money then decided to retire here. It cost him seven million.'

'Wow,' said Al.

'But he really likes cats. He's got about a hundred and fifty and they totally wrecked the place.'

'That's fascinating, man,' said Al.

On the way back the guys did some shopping, but when they got back to the boat there was a small issue that needed fixing. They dropped the shopping on the quayside and Tony got on with the job. It's testament to the honesty of the people of Stornoway that after six hours the shopping was still there.

It's still a working port but the days of the herring industry are gone. The only reminder is a statue of the Herring Girls on the dock. Throughout the trip at many ports there had been plaques or statues commemorating this industry.

At dinner that night another kangaroo court was called. Yanto's personal admin had been deemed to be too messy and you can't have mess on a boat. Shaun donned his admiral's hat to dispense justice.

'I hereby declare that Yanto has broken the articles of *Spirit* on personal admin. Therefore he must, for twenty-four hours, carry a reminder to be tidier,' Shaun declared.

Yanto was handed a ladies' gold handbag to go with his pink Para beret.

Tony's Story

I was conceived in Saltash, born in Plymouth, then straight back across the Tamar to Cornwall for my first pasty. I'm definitely Cornish.

Grew up in Saltash, one brother, one sister and me. My brother is the eldest by a year, then me, then my sister. We all went to the same local school. Mum and Dad are still together. I had a lovely childhood full of sunny days.

My dad was in the Navy. He got my gran to lie and say he was older than he was so he could join up at 15. He ended up being a pinkie, the ones that service all the satellite communications, as opposed to a greenie, who do household electrics.

My grandad was in the Army, in the artillery. He was born in 1908 so he saw the First World War, then when he was older and joined up, he fought through Tobruk and finally ended up being in the standing force in Germany.

There was not much to do in Saltash so me and my brother went to join the Army cadets, but my dad wouldn't let my brother join up because he thought he was too clever to be cannon fodder.

My first job when I left school was as a gardener, working at Ince Castle for Lady Boyd. I was doing an apprenticeship so I went to college once a week. I used to fix everything at the college when it broke, so they offered me a place on their agricultural engineering scheme. I still had military leanings so I applied to the college scheme and the Army at the same time, and made a pledge to myself that whatever came back first was what I would do.

The Army got back to me one day before the college, so I signed up. I signed up in Plymouth, and the kind gentleman in recruitment advised me: 'You need to join your local regiment.' But he joined me up to the Devon and Dorset Regiment rather than a Cornish regiment.

I went off to do my basic training. My dad was really pleased, being ex-Navy. I think my brother was a bit jealous, though. I joined up for the Gulf War, the first one, but by the time I had passed out it was pretty much over. My first posting was to Werl in Germany and the first job I was given was to clean out the Warrior tanks that had come back from the Gulf War.

In 1993 I was sent to Northern Ireland for Operation Banner. Turf Lodge was a pretty sketchy place to work in. You'd be offered a cup of tea by someone who looked just like your grandmother, yet when you'd moved off they would notice where you'd gone to and ring up the local militia to dob you in. Even so, I enjoyed it far more than sitting in a camp in Germany with not enough to do. We were always hyper-vigilant, for the full six months. We were relieved afterwards by the Marines but I stayed on a little bit longer to do the clean-up, so when I got back to Germany all the waggons had already been filled, everyone had been allocated a role, and I was sent down to a sailing club.

'You're from Cornwall, you'll know how to sail,' the OC [Officer Commanding] told me.

I didn't have a fucking clue how to sail, but I just said, Yes, sir.

So off I went to Mohnesee Sailing Club, where I stayed for three years, doing adventure sailing for the Army when they came down to chill out. It was a ridiculously hilarious time. We had finished fixing the yachts one year and the summer season was coming on, so I approached the boss and asked if I could take all the lads down to the bar on the other side of the lake, just to get them out. I couldn't drive but one of the lads could, so we borrowed the minibus and off we went. It was an American-themed restaurant and outside was this eight-foot carving of a Cherokee Indian. Well, the lads all got pissed up, we played pool and had a great time. I went up to pay the bar bill, and when I came back out the Cherokee Indian was in the lake having a swim. They had also pinched a wickerwork table and chairs and they were hidden in the back of the van.

The lad who had agreed to drive, and had promised to stay sober, hadn't, so when he pulled out he drove back on the wrong side of the road.

'I've never driven overseas drunk before,' he pleaded.

The next morning I was woken by the boss. We walked outside and the manager of the bar was there.

'Where are my table and chairs?' he asked.

The boss looked at me. I wasn't going to dob the boys in, so I claimed ignorance. We walked through the accommodation block. I was terrified they were going to find them. In the meantime someone had painted then army green. 'Can't be them, they're ours.'

Later that year I was trying to get ready for a Christmas do and I couldn't do up my collar. When I went home on leave, my mum, who was a nurse, said my neck needed looking at. Back in Germany I went to see the MO [Medical Officer]. He couldn't decide what the lump was so put me on a course of physio. I also had some electric shock therapy. I was fit, running every day.

After six months the lump had grown and I went off to the British Military Hospital. They gave me a biopsy, then I found I was being cas-evaced back to the UK, to Gosport. I still didn't know what was going on. I certainly didn't know what was wrong with me.

Well, until a RAF Wing Commander came in, rattled the obs at the bottom of my army bedstead and said, 'Not looking good, laddie. Cancer.'

That's how I got told I had cancer. I was 24 years old.

I was posted home and put on a course of chemotherapy. I was being treated in a civilian hospital. The chemotherapy worked and I was told the cancer was in remission.

I was engaged at the time to the daughter of a sergeant but that didn't work out. Her mother told her I'd never recover. No one had spoken to me from the forces for eight months, so I signed off. I went up to Lowestoft to do boat building, where I met a guy who owned a sailing engineering company in Plymouth, so I went to work for him. I worked on submarines, type 23 frigates, HMS *Bulwark* and the like. I then went to work on superyachts. Sailed all over: Antigua, Gibraltar, Italy. I was the chief engineer. Life was good.

Then a few years later, totally out of the blue, I got a letter from the Army telling me I had been called up to go as a standing force to Bosnia. I wanted to go, so off I went to Chilwell in Nottinghamshire for the two weeks to ensure eligibility. I did the first couple of days then on day three went to see the MO.

We did all the usual checks, 'Cough, please, sir,' then he started to ask me questions.

'Anything else you need to tell me?'

'Well, I used to have cancer,' I replied.

His face went a bit red and he ripped up my notes and that was the end of that.

After a while the mental side of things started to drive me mad. I was getting flashbacks of Ireland, people getting kneecapped. When you are walking through the centre of Belfast and hear gunshots, everyone stupidly runs towards them. The RUC guy we were with advised: 'Steer away, carry on walking.'

There was a guy, face down on his drive, his wife and daughter standing in the doorway. The Ulster Volunteer Force had just kneecapped him twice.

Right in the middle of Belfast city centre one of my mates got shot. He lost his eye but he survived. I just remember shouting to get FFDs [First Field Dressings] off people to save him, helping to put FFDs into his face. But what caused the flashbacks wasn't these experiences. While we were there we ended up sometimes having to take kids away from their families because they weren't looking after them. It was a weird role to have, really depressing. I found two kids wrapped up in curtains just to keep warm. They were covered in their own shit. Fucking awful. How can anyone treat their own kids like that? I just don't know.

I'd got back with the girl who had left me. About eight years later she had got in contact and said she had been thinking about me, so we got married, bought a house and that. When I had my two daughters, it brought all this back. I split up with my wife and left the family home.

It started to get worse so I ended up talking to psychiatrists and therapists organised by Help for Heroes. I did that EDMR [Eye Movement Desensitisation and Reprocessing] thing. The guy who runs Help for Heroes in Plymouth got me to register as homeless and join their Band of Brothers scheme. They also told me they had put me forward for Engineer on *Spirit* for the Turn to Starboard Round Britain Challenge leaving in a week's time.

I came down and met Shaun. I could tell he was a genuine guy, so I packed up and off we went.

08

HEADING BACK SOUTH

'We may brave human laws, but we cannot resist natural ones'

Jules Verne, Twenty Thousand Leagues
Under the Sea

AT 9AM ON 6 JULY, *SPIRIT* slipped her lines to head off to Skye. The weather was good and all souls on board were safe and well. One uncontrollable, unavoidable element of a sailing trip, however, is the weather. So far, apart from a couple of squalls and a few mild downpours, it had been mild. On many occasions it would have been preferable to have a bit more wind. But now Poseidon, being the contrary sea god he is, thought it was time for a blow-out.

At midday the weather report issued a storm warning. To be safe, a course change was decided and *Spirit* had an unplanned stop at anchorage in Loch Shell, a good holding only 27 miles west of Stornoway, safe as houses. Apparently back in the 1800s the owners of the Lewis Estates had got court orders to throw all the local crofters off the island. They had been spreading rumours of sheep-stealing and the like to get sympathy for the proposed eviction. Cleverly, the locals decide that rather than send a group of angry blokes to remonstrate, they'd send a group of wives. While the gents lit up a pipe and leant on a peat stack, their wives did the business. When the sheriff and his motley crew arrived they were set upon with cries in Gaelic of: 'Cut his trouser braces!'

In this way they sent the sheriff and his mob packing. Luckily a year later the law changed so the crofters were left in peace, with just the legend of the Heroines of Loch Shell.

With oilies you do have a kind of braces, so beware this isle if you're fixed on evicting anyone.

Back on board everyone was enjoying the warmth of the galley and all were down below when a Geordie accent broke from above.

'Guys, you wanne git up here and check this oot, man,' Al called through the doghouse hatch.

We all came up and looked over the side to discover that *Spirit* was surrounded by jellyfish, hundreds of thousands of them. Not having a jellyfish expert on hand, we'll never know which ones they were, just that they were gloopy and quite calming.

Loch Shell was a great place to duck the storm. Next morning the weather seemed good, so we hand-winched the anchor up and got back on course. Pretty quickly after coming out of the safety of the loch, the sea state started to change. The swells increased and it became quite choppy. There is a way of standing on a deck when it is rolling. It's all about letting your knees bend and rolling with the boat, and it's great for the core muscles. This only works to a point, however. The wind speed was increasing so at 11am the foresail came down and it was engine power only.

Spirit can handle pretty much anything. She had already proved that while traveling up to London the previous January during a force 10. The crew, however, were a little squishier.

'I don't feel too well, mate,' said Tony.

'You're going a bit green, bud,' said Chris, laughing.

It was true, the first hues of green had started appearing on Tony's face. He managed to continue his shift on the wheel but as soon as it was time to hand it to someone else, it was game over for him. It has to be said in his defence that he would get up for each shift, manage his 20 minutes on the helm then scarper back to his bunk to ride it out.

He wasn't the only one, he just had it the worst.

The sea was now crashing over the bow and it was getting more and more difficult to stay standing. All of us were clipped on. One wave hit the starboard with a huge jolt and sent Clive off his feet, his arse landing painfully on one of the deck eyes that jut up out of the deck.

He lay there. Dan stood over him.

'That's a dead leg if I've ever seen one. Don't worry, I'm not going to move you, just stop you washing away,' he said to a prostrate Clive, who was dealing with the first bolts of pain.

All he got for a reply was a feeble, 'OK.'

The weather got to such a stage that most were sent below – including Clive with an enormous bruise – with just a couple of old sweats on deck to minimise further dramas. The sea state started to improve. *Spirit* was now edging into the relative safety of the waters between the northern tip of the Isle of Skye and the mainland by Loch Torridon. I think everyone remembers that word from school, when the geography teacher would try to enthuse you about 500-million-year-old mountains.

As the boat became more stable it allowed Dan to start planning for what was to be the next mini challenge on the trip: sailing under Skye Bridge. Skye Bridge connects the Isle of Skye with the mainland at Eilean Ban, spanning Loch Ash. It's a toll bridge and one story claims that any day when Germany beats England at football, German-made cars get free passage.

For *Spirit* the issue was a balance between high tide, reducing the breathing space between the top of the mast and the bridge, and having the tide behind us rather than against us.

It was a race against time as once the tide turned it would be 7 knots on the nose and *Spirit* wouldn't be going anywhere. The almanac, paper, pen and calculator came out. Dan did his calculations and then Chris checked them. It seemed there was over a metre spare. What's the problem? But, just to be sure, they got a piece of string for some practical checking, hoisted it to the top of the mast, took a reading, then dropped another piece to the waterline and measured that. The calculations were right.

Time for a briefing. The crew were called together so everyone knew what was going on. Dan pulled out his little sketch to explain the next bit of fun. On his drawing was a shivering stick man on the back of *Spirit*.

'That's me shitting myself,' said Dan.

There was also a character on the bridge.

'That's Tamsin hanging a fender over the side,' he continued.

As *Spirit* approached the bridge, Tony was on the wheel, Clive on the bow, and everyone else looking up.

Looking up from the deck as you go under a bridge, you have no sense of space and no ability to judge if there is clearing or not. Shaun sidled up to Dan.

'I hope you've got your calculations right,' he said, teasing.

He did. *Spirit* passed under with about 3 metres clearance – or maybe just a fag paper if you want to create a little more drama.

Another kangaroo court had been called and it was decided that Chris had committed some infraction or other needing justice. His punishment was to have to play Frozen Top Trumps with anyone whenever they wanted. He was to drop what he was doing day or night. This might not seem too bad but on a ship that operates twenty-four hours a day, with blokes who like nothing more than ribbing each other, it was a stroke of genius.

Chris would be happily snoring away in the middle of the night in his bunk when he would get a light shake.

'Fancy a game of Top Trumps, mate?' a mischievous shipmate would ask.

Al had also been receiving a bit of incoming. One morning everyone was sitting around the saloon. Someone had kindly made boiled eggs and they were sitting in a bowl for everyone to take one when they wanted.

Al lent over and grabbed one. He rolled it around in his hands, getting to know this new wondrous food.

Everyone by now was watching and waiting.

Al went to eat it, shell and everything.

'No, Al, you have to peel them,' Russ shouted just in time.

Everyone else groaned, the fun spoiled.

'I'd have let me eat it, man,' Al said gamely.

When Clive had joined in Newcastle he had selected a bunk right up in the bow. The bunks there are closer together than the others as they follow the shape of the ship and bend inwards, but as they are right up the far end, they are not in a walkway. Sensibly, he thought he'd not be bothered too much by passing traffic and have a relatively quiet time.

What he hadn't factored in was that opposite him was Al, captain of the Round Britain snoring team.

'I'd wake up and there would be Al, his arse out, with that little tattoo on it of the bloke looking over the wall. He'd just fart in my face and roll over. One night I woke up and we were both facing the same way, our faces were literally millimetres apart. I'd have thought he was trying to kiss me if it wasn't for the racket that told me he was asleep. If I had my choice again I'd have picked another bunk.'

As *Spirit* approached Tobermory, a town lying on the northern tip of the Isle of Mull, the harbourmaster advised over the radio to moor off a lifeboat buoy. To get into town, therefore, it was into the tender and a water taxi to land.

The members of the crew who had young kids were quite excited to be arriving here. It's where the kids' programme *Balamory* is set. In the show, I'm told, various characters live in different colour houses. When you first see the seafront at Tobermory it really is quite engaging: it has houses all painted in various colours. Yellow next to blue, pink next to red, and so on. It is a wonderful scene, almost Mediterranean in its palette. Bang in the middle is the town church, one of the few buildings in a more sombre style. All of this stands out dramatically against the trees behind.

Wandering along Main Street we saw that most of the buildings are shops, pub and restaurants, with a fair few scuba-diving shops. It would seem that diving is popular here because there are lots of shipwrecks nearby. The most celebrated story tells of a shipwreck that no one seems to have actually found yet. The story goes that back in the 1500s England and Spain were engaged in one of their many disagreements. King Philip of Spain put together his huge armada and, after Drake gave them a thumping, many pulled into the east coast of Scotland and some into Ireland to get supplies. The Tobermory legend claims that one of these ships came into the harbour looking for assistance. It was duly given, but there was some kind of payment argument and somehow the ship blew up from its own gunpowder. It was either a treasure ship or a troop ship, but whatever it was, it doesn't seem to want to be found.

There's another whisky distillery here. It would have been rude not to visit so some brave volunteers went off to sample their wares.

As the evening arrived everyone from the three boats got together in one of the pubs. It was a great chance for everyone to share stories about the last few days and about what they had been up to during the day in town. An Irish band had flown in from Donegal and with just a few basic instruments set the pub alive. In usual folk style, they didn't have a set list. Instead, the audience were involved.

'Irish Rover,' someone would shout.

They would go straight into the song, and kept going like that for hours. For us, this was the charm of dropping into faraway places with no real idea what to expect.

Spirit slipped her lines at 0930 hours the next day and made her way out of Tobermory, passing Calve Island that sits just outside, quietly protecting the harbour. We bore south-southeast into the channel that has the Isle of Mull on the starboard and the mainland on the port side, which would take *Spirit* all the way to her next destination. First, a sail to Oban. Wind conditions after a couple of hours became perfect to get the full sail plan into action, so in order the foresail, mainsail, staysail and gib went up. A month ago it would have taken a fair while to do this. Now it took only 27 minutes to have all the sails up catching wind and driving *Spirit* along. After *Spirit* emerged from the channel, Loch Linnie opened up on the port. This large body of water takes you all the way to Fort William, the town at the foot of Ben Nevis, the highest mountain in the UK. Beyond there runs the Caledonian Canal, which was once considered for the challenge. Another day, another trip, perhaps.

It was a relatively short sail to Oban. At 5pm the anchor was holding well, not in Oban itself but just across in Ardentrive Bay on the eastern side of the island Kerrara. Just an 800-metre tender ride to the town, if the tender worked. It didn't. Dan and Chris set about trying to fix the outboard. In the meantime one of the locals lent the team a tender to enable Dan to get everyone ferried across to the mainland.

While Dan was preparing to go back to *Spirit*, a family of Italian tourists got his attention.

'How much to take us over to our boat?' the man asked, obviously thinking that this was a taxi.

'Only four pounds,' Dan replied, cheekily.

So all the family jumped in and had a lift to their boat. When they went to pay, Dan told them it was free.

Maybe now in some Italian guidebook it tells you that water taxis are free in Oban.

Throughout the trip, aside from the occasional chances to get ashore and interact with other people, every person was bound to the boat. That's a huge amount of time spent in a closed environment with nowhere really to escape to. At night, on deck, you can grab a few moments, or in your own bunk space with the tiny curtain pulled across for respite. You can read a book or watch a movie on a laptop to take you away in mind if not in body.

Even though as soldiers everyone had experienced living on top of other people, those days were in the past. Since then, many if not all on board had been through dark periods in their life. Just like anyone, everyone had bad days; some had few, some had many. Does it make it worse or better if you are surrounded by people who suffer as well? In hindsight, I think it's better. There is a tolerance, an understanding; yet another weird common bond you share.

There was a method on board to deal with it. Whoever was having that bad day, the rest either gave them a bit of support or left them alone. Each person deals with demons in a different way. With all that and so many other variables thrown into the mix, the desire not to let each other down and to make sure things were done on time remained paramount. Not one person missed their stag (their watch).

Russ's Story

I'm Warrington, Cheshire, born and bred. There's just me and my big brother. He's seven years older than me and I always looked up to him.

He left school just as I joined but he had a good reputation there so the teachers looked kindly upon me. He was both sporty and clever. I remember I joined a local fencing team. I was doing OK at it, then he came down to have a look and beat everyone in the club. I joined a hockey team. After four years I'd managed to make it into the first team. He turns up, week two, yep, he's in the first team. He now runs the local fire station as he decided to go into the Fire Service when he left school. But I guess I'm the more people person of the two of us.

My dad was in the RAF; my granddad was in the Royal Engineers. I wasn't sure whether to follow my brother or my dad, so I applied to both the Army and Fire Service.

I'd wanted to join at 15 but my dad said no, so I did my A levels at college first. I was 17 and Dad still didn't want me to join.

'Well, if you don't sign, he'll only go and do it when he's eighteen,' Mum said. She was right.

Dad's only comment was that I wasn't to join the Infantry. He had worked a bit with the Hereford lads in his RAF career so he was just looking out for me.

I applied to the Engineers and the Signals and went down to Lichfield to do my selection. I remember doing the 1.5-mile run and one of my trainers came off halfway through. I was too scared to stop to pick it up because I didn't want to fail so I ran the rest of it one-shoed. I needn't have worried, I came in second in under 8 minutes. In fact, I had time to go back get my trainer and still qualify.

As I had applied for the Signals, there was a maths test. The questions got increasingly hard the longer the test went on, and I had heard that they marked backwards. They would check and see what was the last question you got right and that would be your mark. So I worked backwards, only answered three questions. I thought I'd probably messed up but I got top grades.

I then went to Bassingbourn to do my basic training. It was a mixed group of cap badges and the troop above us were all female. It was 1995 and the Army was experimenting with non-differentiated gender roles. It was really interesting seeing them pit the two cadres against each other.

In week 9 I slipped and got injured and was put back a squad while I recovered. I was now in a fully REME [Royal Electrical and Mechanical Engineers] unit and it was the first time I realised the camaraderie you get in a formed unit: the joking about, the mutual support, the friendships that had been formed through shared experiences.

I passed out on my eighteenth birthday and went home for Xmas leave. When I went back to my original unit in Blandford I caught up with the blokes who were on my course. They had been kicking their heels, pulling guard duty, and I just waltzed in and went straight on to my technical training. I spent a year at college learning electronics so I was OK. At Leconfield I learnt to drive. This being the Army I didn't learn in a car then progress, it was straight into an HGV and off driving around the streets of Hull.

I was posted to 14th Signals. This is the only electronic warfare unit in the Army, so whenever the Army goes anywhere, 14th goes too. At the end of 1996 I got sent to Bosnia. I wasn't in a formed unit, so everyone was from differing places, the Navy, GCHQ, even some civvies. Before we got there the Dutch electronic warfare team had been executed, which obviously made it a bit scary. We were responsible for tracking down the guerrilla criminals who were still cutting up kids and burning Christians. We liaised with the types on the ground who went in to pick these guys up. We called them PIFWICs: people indicted for war crimes. You really felt like you were doing some good. It was a brilliant tour.

After that tour I went to Warminster to the infantry school training wing, teaching signals to infantry guys. While we were there the Army was running Operation FIST: Future Infantry Soldier Technology. So we were always wired up with loads of kit from the movies, shooting around corners and the like, although the best thing was dicking around with Napoleon's duelling pistols. He'd given them to some old soldier when he was in St Helena.

In September 2001 I went 30 Signal Regiment, nicknamed the Globetrotters and considered prestigious. From there I was deployed for pretty much the rest of my career. When the Twin Towers happened we were on 24-hour readiness. The pagers went off just before Christmas so we rushed in ready to be sent as part of the spearhead. But they decided they didn't want to send us just in case something bigger went off.

I did a tour in Iraq, then I went to Sierra Leone. I found it weird arriving at the airport and because we were white just being waved through. I found that really uncomfortable. But I was reunited with a lot of old mates. We had the same role as Bosnia, lifting warlords. One bloke was called Sam 'Mosquito'

Bockarie. He had quite a career path: disco dancer, hairdresser, then infamous warlord lobbing arms off people.

I was on Larium, the malaria tablets, there, and I dreamt that I had killed someone in Basra and buried them. For quite a while afterwards I was convinced it was true.

I went back to Iraq rebuilding all the schools around Basra, just a bunch of Siggies [Signals] driving around in a softskin Land Rover. We felt quite exposed. I hate to say it but we aren't like the infantry in this kind of situation. We are not trained for or used to coming into direct contact with the enemy. A truck came down the road and my Spidey-sense went mad, so we bugged out [retreated]. We were always so hyper-vigilant.

We heard later that the truck had been blown up by the Army as it was a threat. I'd rather go through the hassle of moving fifty times and being wrong than staying put and being wrong.

I came out in 2006 after Operation Herrick 9. I'd started to have political opinions about where we were and what we were doing and it was affecting me. I got a job in a construction company refurbishing Marriot Hotels, then something started to go wrong. I couldn't put my finger on it. I couldn't sleep. I was having night terrors and waking up in sweats. Being on a building site was reminding me of the past, the smells, dust everywhere. I quit my job and set up on my own.

I went to see my doctor, just gave my list of usual little woes. I was on my way out when she stopped me and looked at me.

'You need to tell me what's really wrong,' she said.

I broke down in tears. That was the start of my recovery. I got referred to the mental health team and they signposted me to the North West Veterans Mental Health Team. They were outstanding. While I was waiting for treatment they gave me loads of soft skills courses, so when I did start the treatment I was ready. It taught me to have a routine and to stick to it. I have a wife and three kids so it's important for all of us.

The team linked me up with a local charity who got me to join Band of Brothers, the Help for Heroes charity. It was from them that I got the email about sailing with Turn to Starboard.

My first taste of sailing was on the familiarisation trip. I hadn't been near to or spoken to anyone military for a while; I had kept away from them. I drove down to Falmouth and sat outside the office. Then I drove away, cried for 45 minutes and phoned the office, hoping no one would answer. But Tamsin answered and so I went back. She introduced me to everyone. I sat down and told Shaun my story, then he shared his.

Then I went sailing. I loved the instant feeling of being with people doing the same thing, all working together, being out at sea. It gives my brain a chance to rest.

Everything else can go fuck itself.

09

WHISKY GALORE

'Because it's there'

George Mallory

SLIPPING LINES AT 11AM was a well-deserved late start for the crew. The tender had now been fixed and *Spirit* could carry on with her journey heading on a bearing of 240 degrees, passing north of the island of Garbh Eileach and heading southwest to the inner Hebridean islands of Colonsay and Oronsay. By 2pm the weather was fair and all the sails were up, and by 9pm she was nicely tucked into an anchorage just east of the southerly of the two islands, Oronsay.

The larger island, Colonsay, has a population of only 124; Oronsay a shy eight. But don't imagine these far-flung and scarcely populated islands lack their share of interests. Colonsay is the smallest island in the world with its own microbrewery, named, appropriately, Colonsay Brewery, a safe brand name, but one that also shows confidence. It was also the home of a certain John McNeil, born in 1831. He became a major general in the British Army, serving in various roles before becoming equerry to Queen Victoria, no less. His most prestigious accomplishment was to receive the highest award that any soldier can receive, the Victoria Cross, the award that was introduced by the Queen in 1856. At the time he was a lieutenant in Bengal Light Infantry, who were taking part in the New Zealand Wars, which shows how global and widespread the British Army was in those days.

His citation reads:

For the valour and presence of mind which he displayed in New Zealand, on the 30th of March, 1864, which is thus described by Private Vesper, of the Colonial Defence Force.

Private Vosper states that he was sent on that day with Private Gibson, of the same Force, as an escort to Major (now Lieutenant- Colonel) McNeill, Aide-de-Camp to Lieutenant-General Sir Duncan Cameron. Lieutenant-Colonel McNeill was proceeding to Te Awamutu on duty at the time.

On returning from that place, and about a mile on this side of Ohanpu, this Officer, having seen a body of the enemy in front, sent Private Gibson back to bring up Infantry from Ohanpu, and he and Private Vosper proceeded leisurely to the top of a rise to watch the enemy.

Suddenly they were attacked by about 50 natives, who were concealed in the fern close at hand. Their only chance of escape was by riding for their lives, and as they turned to gallop, Private Vosper's horse fell and threw him.

The natives thereupon rushed forward to seize him, but Lieutenant-Colonel McNeill, on perceiving that Private Vosper was not following him, returned, caught his horse, and helped him to mount. The natives were firing sharply at them, and were so near that, according to Private Vosper's statement, it was only by galloping as hard as they could that they escaped. He says that he owes his life entirely to Lieutenant-Colonel McNeill's assistance, for he could not have caught his horse alone, and in a few minutes must have been killed.

In this barren and wild land lies his tomb, a recipient of few visitors. That such a tiny place can produce such a hero, and have such a link to the richness of British military history, was extraordinary. The smaller island Oronsay may not have such a military link, but as a yin needs its yang it can boast one of the most famous names in religious history. St Columba, the Irish saint, landed here. He was looking for a place to start a new abbey but as he could still see

Ireland from here he decided to go further and finally decided upon Iona. He made it his base, building his abbey and becoming a major force in bringing Christianity to Scotland.

We were able to make another late start as it was only about 35 nautical miles to the next destination, Port Ellen, on the Isle of Islay. We first crossed back east towards the Isle of Jura, *Spirit*, *Quivira II* and *September* calmly sailing in a meandering column through the straits, which are half a nautical mile wide with the more mountainous and foreboding Jura to port and the pleasant Islay to starboard. Islay is famous for a few things, none more important than whisky. In fact, it's really famous for whisky, so it seemed a suitable place for yet another tour. Al and a couple of the guys went off to sample more of the amber delights, while others went through making *Spirit* secure. Whereas only a month ago the likes of Shaun and Dan had to suggest the jobs that need doing, now it was all second nature for the crew.

The word 'whisky' had by now been on the lips of the crew for a few days, both in sound and in taste. What is all the fuss about? The word is a translation of 'water', percolating from the Latin 'aqua vitae' or 'water of life' through various versions of Gaelic until we get 'whisky'. If the name is spelt 'whiskey' the drink comes from Ireland (or the States); as *Spirit* didn't get to the Emerald Isle there shall be no use of the extra vowel here.

The distillation process used in making whisky was first employed for the production of perfumes to adorn the ladies and gentleman of the Near East many a millennia ago in Babylonia. Ancient Greek sailors used the process to turn seawater into drinking water, seriously missing a trick while doing so. They were probably too busy conquering the known world to sit around and wait for a drop of the good stuff.

Grapes in northern Europe were quite scarce due to the climate. In fact, they still are, so at the time the preferred item to ferment, the one that was to hand, was grain. It's fundamentally why Northern Europeans are more likely to prefer beer or whisky to wine.

Almost all the desired distilled products still came from the continent, especially from France. Those wily French were exporting Cognac to pretty much every major person of note in the UK, lords, ladies and the like. Meanwhile the monks in the UK were quietly and merrily spreading the word accompanied with their golden liquid unhindered on a minor scale until two major historical events occurred. First, Henry VIII dissolved the monasteries, making a fair few monks jobless and forcing them to look for something to do other than spread religion. Not long after Scotland and England merged, England then needed taxes to pay for various wars overseas. (Did we mention the Spanish Armada?) The monks decided to go underground, only working at night when the darkness masked the smoke rising from their illegal stills. This is where we get the word 'moonshine' for illicit liquor, a word we generally associate with the US prohibition. These cheeky chaps used to smuggle their illicit booze in coffins, happily keeping supplies under their pulpits.

An unusual event that put whisky into the forefront of the drinks industry of the time was the nineteenth-century attack on the vines in France by a small pest called phylloxera. It destroyed grapes and, therefore, damaged the successful cognac industry, and suddenly there was a demand for another source of tipple. An unknown Scot, whose involvement in whisky cannot be understated, decided one day to put home-grown whisky in the empty cognac barrels that had been imported from France and were now sitting around. The result was widespread access to a new wonderful drink and everyone gave a sigh of relief.

In 1823 it became legal again to make whisky in Scotland. An even bigger sigh of relief.

The story has one more twist though. In the US in 1920, under pressure from the Temperance Society, the US government made the decision to ban the import of whisky, to coincide with its federal ban on the sale of alcohol. But two organisations benefitted. First it was deemed legal to sell whisky for medicinal purposes, and that helped a fledgling drugstore company called Walgreen to make a few dollars (it is now the biggest drug distributor in the US). Another a small organisation could not believe its luck that the US government had dumped a huge business in its lap. It was called the Mafia.

At 5pm the anchor was down and *Spirit* was secured just in sight of Port Ellen, the main port on the island. On the western tip of Kilnaughton Bay, the natural inlet that houses Port Ellen, is Carraig Fhada lighthouse. By now *Spirit* had seen a fair few of these, but this one was like no other. It consists of two tall square buildings, the larger seeming to offer the smaller protection from the crashing waves. The lighthouse was built by Walter Frederick Campbell in memory of his wife Eleanor. Indeed, it was Walter who established Port Ellen, which is also named after his wife.

Not bad getting a whole town named after you. The Campbells were a big deal in these parts for most of modern Scottish history and bought the island in the early nineteenth century for what was quite an amount at the time, a princely twelve grand. They developed various industries on the island, such as copper mining, and obviously whisky. Whisky isn't made here any longer, but the island does provide the malt that is the key ingredient.

Walter got into a bit of debt, to the tune of eight hundred thousand pounds, before the management of the island was taken off him and passed to an accountant, who subsequently sold the island for half a million to a man described as a commoner. A commoner with an uncommon amount of cash, it would seem.

Visually Port Ellen is similar to Tobermory, except that all the houses here are stonewashed white. They all sit on the waterfront and when reflected in the water below the place almost looks like a sweet, hidden Mediterranean gem.

It was Tamsin's birthday while we were at anchor here, so the chaps clubbed together to get her a gift and Russ made lemon drizzle cake – everyone's favourite cake, surely? Everyone from the three boats crowded into *Spirit*'s saloon with people eating off knees, heads and anything to hand, all to say Happy Birthday till Tamsin went red with embarrassment. She is a wonderful combination of utterly capable and shy. She will make someone a wonderful partner – if they can manage to get past her bodyguards.

'I should be out with a bunch of 25-year-old girls getting drunk, not fixing gearboxes and calming you lot down,' she said.

It was also the first anniversary of Dan's involvement with Turn to Starboard. What a great place to celebrate. During the day a group had been over to have wander around the island and had found a memorial to fallen comrades, where they spent a few moments in remembrance. On the walk back they discovered that someone had built a gymkhana course on the beach for Shaun to jump over. Sadly no photos survive.

The beaches of Islay have bleached yellow sand and clear blue water. The little group slowly split up, each finding their own individual spot on the beach to relax, collect their thoughts and recuperate. On the tender for the trip back, everyone crowded into a selfie to send back to Ellen in the Turn to Starboard office. This amazing lady was responsible not only for project-managing all this but also for organising press to come and visit *Spirit* whenever she docked. Meanwhile, in a shorefront pub, Yanto was chatting to the locals, as is his way, slightly rocking from one leg to another, pint in hand. Dan sneaked up behind him and, as Yanto put his weight on his real leg, unclipped the prosthetic. Yanto swayed back, found the leg unattached and did an unexpected parachute roll on the floor.

'You buggers!'

Please note that no royal marines or paras were hurt in the making of this challenge, just the creation of eternal banter.

Port Ellen had been a wonderful rest but it was time to move on. To get into the next harbour at the right tide it was necessary to leave in the afternoon and pull an overnighter. It was time to leave Scotland, its islands and wonderful people behind. *Spirit* had spent eighteen days in Scottish waters, but with her most important engagement to get to in Liverpool in a few days' time it was necessary to get a few more nautical miles under her keel.

Our next destination was the Isle of Man. The passage would be pretty simple, sticking between a heading of 140 and 165 degrees until we reached Peel harbour on the island's northwestern coast. We passed the Mull of Kintyre, whose name will always be remembered by people of a certain age because of the song written by Paul

McCartney, who stood on a windy hill singing 'Oh Mull of Kintyre' for what seemed like my entire childhood.

Ireland was on the starboard and so *Spirit* sailed majestically between the two down through the North Channel. The channel here is 22 miles wide, which is only just over a mile wider than the English Channel. It was once the domain of privateers sneaking around and stealing from commercial ships passing through the funnelled waters. It wasn't going to be too long before some strapping chap decided to swim it. Up stepped such a strapping lad, Tom Bowyer, a Nottingham-born man who had served in the Royal Navy. During his service he rescued a drowning man, for which gallantry he was awarded the Royal Humane Society Medal. Hang on a minute, haven't we heard this before from Captain Webb? Well, yes, they both swam trying to save a chap and got the same medal.

Earlier in his life, Tom was so poor at fast swimming he was nicknamed 'carthorse' by his unkind buddies, but after finding distance swimming he became 'Torpedo Tom'. Torpedo swam the English Channel twice, once even attempting the return swim, but he was foiled by the weather. It was ten years later, in 1947, that Tom attempted the North Channel and became the first person to do it successfully, in freezing waters and with his feet nibbled by a shoal of herring. He finally emerged from the water to be greeted by a cheerful Scottish police officer.

He really was a superstar of the time, but after a while he decided to hang up his trunks.

'I'm going to put my swimming trunks on a pole and when I find a place where no one knows what they are, that's the place for me,' he said, puzzlingly.

Swimming types say that this is a far harder challenge than the channel. To be honest, the water did look cold.

Spirit passed this famous crossing and arrived in Peel harbour midmorning. By now the standard operating procedure was like clockwork. Yanto and Clive would make a list of items needed and sally off to get replenishments. Shaun and Tamsin would finish up the jobs that need covering on *Spirit*, then continue liaising with Ellen and the charity back in Falmouth. The crew would get the *Spirit* in order, and then and only then was downtime declared.

The Isle of Man is famous for cats with no tails, the TT race and Nigel Mansell. No one went off specifically to find the famous cats but a couple of the guys got bikes and cycled the TT route, but a bit slower. One thing for sure: this is the only place from which you can see all the nations that form the British Isles. The highest point on the island is Snaefell at a mere 610 metres tall. On the summit is a plaque which, along with compass points, reads:

31 miles to the Mull of Galloway (Scotland)
51 miles to Scafell (England)
66 miles to the Mountains of Mourne (Northern Ireland)
85 miles to Liverpool (England)
97 miles to Dublin (Eire)

It was quite disappointing to find out that Nigel Mansell wasn't actually from the Isle of Man. He was born in Worcestershire and only moved there later in life. But, and it's a big but, guess who does hail from here? Only the Bee Gees. It's true. The Gibb Brothers were born here and there's even a blue plaque on the post office wall in Douglas to prove it. So the 'John Travolta strutting along with his paint pot in hand, medallion out' soundtrack is something that was spawned on the Isle of Man. One of the hardest tests in the world is listening to the first few bars of 'Stayin' Alive' and remaining utterly still.

Tony and Yanto strutted off to go swimming, the local kids mesmerised by the sight of them, this one-legged man and his mate laughing and joking. People would also stop and give us money for the charity, something that had happened everywhere, from the Isle of Wight to the Isle of Man. Throughout this trip the general public were wonderful in their welcome and their treatment of the guys. This was not matched entirely by the way the crew treated each other. It's the same sentiment but it comes in a particular type of forces love. Here's an example.

Yanto, Dan and Clive were sitting in a bar. Clive wasn't drinking but wasn't letting that stop his mischievousness. Yanto was telling stories. Each time he looked away, each of the others would slyly slip a coin into the gap that opens in Yanto's prosthetic leg when he sits.

'What are you two laughing at?' he asked suspiciously.

'Nothing, mate, carry on with your Para stories,' answered Clive.

As the two ageing schoolboys got bolder, the coins got bigger. It was time to leave and they all stood up to make it back to the boat. On the way back, Yanto started to complain.

'My leg is a bit uncomfortable.'

'Better have a look when you get back, mate,' Dan said sympathetically with a knowing look to Clive.

Back on *Spirit*, Yanto sat down and started to unclip his leg. Clive and Dan made sure they were close by for the reveal. As he unclipped his leg, about four pounds fifty came tumbling out, like a man-size buckaroo, to the laughter of both.

'You buggers, that could have hurt!'

'Well, at least you have some money for plasters,' said Clive.

Morale was high, everything was going to plan, *Spirit* was looking after the crew and the crew were looking after her. The last few legs had been mild and the sailing had, if anything, been somewhat easy. But things were about to change. The next leg was to be a different game altogether.

Clive's Story

My family is Cornish and I grew up in Penzance. Two brothers, one older, one younger. The eldest is a Royal Marine and just about to retire after forty-two years' service. My younger brother works in the immigration department. I retired this year after thirty-nine years' Army service.

Three of us brothers grew up having an uneventful, fun childhood. After a few years we moved up country, to Didcot, but we always went back to Cornwall any chance we got. At one stage we had nearly two hundred relatives down there. My father was a locomotive fireman, working the footplates, stoking the engine. Then he became a fireman at a laboratory in a nuclear research establishment. He was there just in case anything went wrong.

At the time I was leaving school, around 15 years old, one of our weekend days out was to jump on the train at Didcot, go into Oxford and go to the cinema. My friend really wanted to join the Army, so I went with him and, while he sat in his interview, I sat in the waiting room.

A guy came out and had a chat with me. 'Are you here to join up, young man?'

'Noooo, just here with a mate,' I answered.

Nonetheless, he sat down with me and went through all the details, and so I went home and told my parents it was what I wanted to do. They let me. I finished my exams and off I went and joined up in 1978 as a junior leader, which was for training recruits who were under 18 years old. Funnily enough, the guy I went in with that day only did three years. I did thirty-nine.

In September 1979 I joined my first regiment, the Royal Artillery, as a gunner, in Larkhill, Wiltshire. But I was a junior rugby player and back in those days there were only two really good rugby gunner regiments, the 7 RHA and 22 Welsh Gunners, so almost immediately I got picked up and went off to 22 regiment in Germany, getting to play loads of rugby.

I was living in the barrack block where you had multiple-man rooms. We had flats that held seventeen people and it was like gang warfare in those days. I remember one day in the shower being shot at with an air rifle, just to see if I was tough enough.

That was where bonding really took place. You lived and you went down as a team. We'd finish work, scrub up and all go out together. It's a far different world now with single-man rooms.

I got sent to Northern Ireland twice, one urban tour which was pretty routine, patrolling Belfast, and a rural tour, which meant you would go on four- to five-day patrols. We were on patrol the day when the Enniskillen bomb went off in 1987. Our section found the largest ever HME [Homemade Explosive] bomb, 3,000 pounds hidden in a silage spreader.

I really grew up on those tours. Apart from the Cold War it was the war of our time. I guess it's like the young lads who recently went off to Afghanistan. It really makes a change to them as soldiers and men. We were in a country right next to our own, where everybody looked the same as us, and you spent six months trying to work who was on whose side. It was the height of the Troubles so there was an incident every single day.

On my first patrol I had to attend a shooting. A 17-year-old lad had been kneecapped, shot in the legs from behind. Apparently he had just been dating the wrong girl.

After that we did tours in Cyprus and the Falklands. Then I was posted to Cardiff as a recruitment sergeant for two years, then went back to my regiment for six months. I got picked for a year-long gunnery tech course, where you come out a Warrant Officer Instructor of Gunnery. I was WO2 at the age of 29 – a sergeant major at that age, it was great. It was a dream posting to be instructing at the school of artillery. In those days the crème de la crème was to be on the gunnery staff as SMIG [Sergeant Major Instructor Gunnery] with a white hat. It designated that I was an expert in my field, be it practical or technical. I became a troop sergeant major, then a battery sergeant major of an air assault battery.

I was disappointed that our regiment didn't get deployed to the Gulf War. We had just got back from Northern Ireland and so they sent another regiment. I then became the RSM of 16 Regiment Royal Artillery at the age of 37, based in Woolwich, London, and also Garrison Sergeant Major. The CO at the time told me

I was more of a modern RSM. I didn't walk around screaming and shouting but spent a lot of time re-educating and having many 'correctional chats'.

'Come here, young man,' I would say. 'Why is it pissing down with rain and you are not wearing your waterproofs?'

'They are in my room, sir,' would be the reply.

There would be a correctional chat so it wouldn't happen again.

Again, fantastic times, being based at the home of the Gunners. We had a great mess. It was like being the landlord of your own pub. What made it was having a bunch of really good sergeant majors working for me who knew what they were doing.

At that time I was seriously considering leaving the Army. I didn't know how I could top this and I was coming to the end of my appointment. Then one day the CO walked into my office.

'I haven't seen your application for commission yet.'

'I haven't put one in, sir,' I replied.

A couple of days later I got a phone call from the adjutant of London District Headquarters telling me I had been requested for an interview with the General Officer Commanding.

I marched in.

'What's this I hear that you haven't applied for a commission?'

'That's right, sir,' I replied.

'Well, you will apply, because you will be successful. Do we understand each other?'

I got my commission as a captain.

So I returned to instructing, teaching the top 5 per cent of the gunners in the Army. It was the plum job for a late-entry officer. I had also requested to complete all the courses that any lieutenant being made up to captain would have to complete. It was a year of courses. Later I was deployed to Afghanistan, which was pre-Herrick, and given an acting rank as major doing a disarmament, disbandment and reintegration role. I spent time reintegrating the people to ensure there weren't any unnecessary power vacuums. We found one guy who had six T62 tanks hidden in a cave, which was his bargaining chip for the other tribes around him. So we had to go around and get the weapons off the other guys.

We were living in a tiny tented camp. We went out in armoured cars, turned up at the village the sneaky beakys had already identified, broke bread with them and gave them $1,500 for a tank. A great role in a lawless time and place. We were forever getting shot at, basically because they didn't know who we were.

Then I went back to the regiment, picked up being a major, went to the States, Egypt and Norway, then off to spend eight months at the Staff College. I did another tour of Afghanistan embedded with the Afghan Army, doing their training and planning. We had several green on blues. I guess I was lucky and managed to duck a bit quicker than others.

After that I was selected to become the first late-entry officer to command a line battery, a great honour. We deployed to Iraq and the Falklands.

Then I was promoted to lieutenant colonel and selected for the WTE [Where Talent Endures] post. These are the punchiest jobs you can do as an officer, working pan Army, pan NATO, writing and planning projects on how we were going to deliver advance force operations worldwide. I've been told I've always been able to see the problem, see it early and cut out the crap. I seem to be able to communicate both verbally and in writing, and get the right people in the room to solve the problem. All these roles involved 18-hour days and this finally took its toll. Every time I walked into an office I was getting another tasking. I'd start work at 7am, work till 7pm, take work home until midnight or 2am then start again for 7am the next day.

I got burnt out. I was hollow. I was put on sick leave and got involved with Help for Heroes to do one of their courses designed to get you ready for life as a civilian. You get lots of pieces of paper on your desk and I filled them out. I must have filled out a form for Turn to Starboard. I got a phone call letting me know I'd been selected for the Round Britain Challenge. I went down to the familiarisation trips and loved it.

10

LIVERPOOL

*'I've never known a better seaman, but as a man, he's a
snake'*

> *Lt Fletcher Christian about Captain Bligh
> in the film,* Mutiny on the Bounty

IT WAS ANOTHER EVENING ANCHOR SLIP. *Spirit*'s
next destination was Liverpool, where the story of her ilk
started and where there was to be quite a celebration to
mark the anniversary. *Spirit* already had a rendezvous with
a local pilot and this meant it was to be another overnighter
for the crew to make it on time. We came back out of the
harbour heading north-northwest then changed course
to 120 degrees to sail down past the southwestern coast
of the Isle of Man. Once *Spirit* passed the Calf of Man,

the small island that sits on the southerly tip, she changed again, heading for Liverpool.

For the next six hours all went well: the weather was good, the sea state was slight. But then the barometer reading started to drop, an indication of reducing air pressure, which can mean, though it does not always, that poor weather is on its way. At 0300 fog started to come in. In the distance the sky was lit by forked bolts of lightning. Shaun and Dan were watching with caution. Safety had always been Shaun's highest priority. During the trip he had given more and more responsibility to his first mate Dan and Dan had stepped up on each occasion, but Shaun was always the senior sailor, there for advice if needed.

To watch a lightning storm from a beach while it cracks and splutters over the sea is to enjoy one of nature's most exhilarating spectacles. Watching the same thing while on a tall ship is somewhat disconcerting. We were not fearful people, but this situation, with nature at its most violent, raised the heartbeats of the crew, for whom it was something of an unknown.

On board was every piece of modern equipment available to a modern seafarer, including conductors to channel the force to the sea if necessary. The weather seemed to be getting closer. Dan called everyone on shift together for a briefing.

'I just want to put you all at ease. I know it looks a bit dramatic, but we have more chance of a whale leaping out of the sea and landing on the deck than of us getting struck by lightning.'

The shift changed and a new crew came on and Dan repeated his comments to the new guys.

The storm continued to approach. The rain started to come down for real and the brightness increased as the lightning got closer. Russ was on the helm. *Whack!* Lightning hit the mast and travelled down and into the water, leaving everyone with a fuzzy feeling and their hair sticking up.

The rain continued but luckily the electrical storm passed. By 0800 *Spirit* was at the bar to collect the harbour pilot. The visibility at the time, however, was poor.

The pilot came on board and once the pleasantries were over Shaun asked him if he wanted to take her in. It was, after all, the relationship between schooners and the Merseyside pilots that had started this journey off.

Clive, who was on the wheel, remarked, 'But watch her, mate, she's a bit slow on reacting.'

'Yeah, all right, mate. I think I'll be OK,' he said, and chuckled.

Modern-day pilots have to go through a long and stringent process to become fully fledged. They will almost certainly have already spent many years sailing and being a deck officer, and will have the appropriate qualifications to work as a captain. Although it differs from place to place, once a sailor decides upon a port of choice he or she will then have six months' training, watching and learning from an experienced pilot. If the candidate passes the examination assessment, he or she is then given the authority of a pilot licence. That's just where it starts. Each size and weight of ship requires a specific licence, so over the next five years the candidate will slowly advance, having annual assessments till they finally become fully authorised.

It showed. The pilot guided *Spirit* beautifully, ferry gliding from one point to another.

'This guy is a ninja,' Dan said, full of respect.

Spirit crept to her mooring right outside the Liverpool Maritime Museum, prime berth for the star of the show.

The plan was to spend a few days here to let the people of Liverpool see *Spirit* and, if they wished, learn about the history that surrounds the pilot service. The Maritime Museum put on a well-researched and thorough exhibition that included the history of the original ships, how the pilot service evolved over the years, and lots of personal stories that brought the facts to life. The crew were given a tour which was fascinating for all of us.

Lots of dignitaries and senior members of the Liverpool pilot community came on board, bolstering an already powerful feeling of achievement.

Over the short period that Turn to Starboard had owned *Spirit*, lots of stories and myths had been circulating, and it was wonderful to have all this laid out by professional researchers in the know. They dispelled a few falsehoods and filled in a few knowledge gaps about what the ships had been used for, how they had received their payment and what life was like aboard. A wonderful exhibition: I hope many people got to see it.

With one of the major legs finished, some of the crew had to leave, but a fresh bunch arrived, including Adrian, an Infanteer who had served with both the Regulars and the Reservists and had had a career in the fire service. They were all willing to patiently and proudly escort the public around *Spirit* so they could see the closest thing available to the real thing.

To the crew, of course, she was the real thing.

Adrian's Story

I was born in Birmingham. I'm now 43 years young. I have an older sister and we grew up in an area on the outskirts of the city. I was lucky to have a good upbringing. My parents were together and I had a very solid family.

No one in my family was in the forces apart from my grandad, who was a medic. He spent his time in India doing his job and, from what he told me, fighting off red ants all the time.

I was quite an average student. Initially I wanted to be an architect, but for some reason I didn't get my subject options, specifically technical drawing, and after that I couldn't be arsed so I just cruised the last two years at school. I decided to join the Army when I left school but my parents advised me that I should get a trade first so I'd have something to fall back on. I did a two-year apprenticeship as a motor mechanic.

I still wanted to join the forces, do something special. I wasn't trying to run away from anything, but I liked the idea of going off and doing my own thing. I wasn't a particularly confident child so I wanted something that would build my confidence and gain me respect. Certain members of my family laughed when I told them I wanted to join up, so I suppose there was maybe a little bit of wanting to prove myself.

I went to the RAF and signed up, did my selection and was all set to be an aircraft technician, but there was a waiting period of 12 months before I could start basic training. I couldn't wait, so I went next door to the Army office. I had the usual score, that whoever is working in recruitment steers you towards whatever they do. The guy was a tank soldier from the Queen's Own Hussars, a Brummie regiment, so I joined as a tank soldier in 1991.

My unit wasn't involved in the Gulf War, so even if I had been earlier I'd have missed it. I went off to Catterick to do my core training, basic, driving and signals, then I went off to join my unit in Germany, where I spent three years altogether. I started off as a driver, then became a gunner, then did some time with recce troop. It was quite a drinking culture. I remember driving a 72-tonne tank under the influence down a range road past RMPs. It was madness, but a brilliant time.

In 1993 I went to Northern Ireland in an infantry role, partly doing patrols in Belfast and then being a guard at the Maze Prison. When I first got to the prison I went on a visitor's trip because I was curious. It was an eye-opener. I was amazed at how plush the place was. Each faction had its own wing. I didn't feel the guards ran the place, more that the prisoners did.

I was young and patrolling Belfast was scary. I look back now after doing tours overseas and think that then we were patrolling around in our own country. The houses were the same, people looked the same, the cars, the traffic signs, a very strange feeling.

I got involved with a girl from Birmingham. She had her own business and life in the UK and she wouldn't move to Germany where I was based, so I went to sign off. The unit tried to keep me, sending me to the elite of the regiment, the recce troop. I did an exercise in Canada and again really enjoyed it. But then I left, and I remember my dad saying, 'Son, you are making the biggest mistake of your life.' But I thought I knew best.

About six months after I got home I split up with the girl. I was going to join back up, but I had applied to the Fire Service and that job came up. I spent seventeen years in the Fire Service in total. Got married, had children.

My brother-in-law was in the TA as an RMP [Royal Military Police] and he got called up for a tour. I was surprised. I didn't think the TA did that. I looked into it and in 2003 I joined up myself. I had looked at an armoured unit but they didn't have much involvement with armoured vehicles so I joined an infantry unit, the West Midlands Regiment/Staffords, which has since become 4 Mercian. I was 30 then, and I fitted into it really well. I volunteered to go to Iraq. I got attached to 1 Staffords and did Telic 6 with them. It was good to be with a regular unit. Some of my TA lot were still old school, a bit of a club.

The Staffords found out I had a track licence so I did a Warrior conversion course, the plan being that I could step in if needed. I ended up spending most of my tour driving Land Rover Snatches then Warriors. It was quite a lively tour. There is a famous news clip of our guys jumping out of a Warrior while it was on fire. I haven't processed that stuff properly yet, but I know it's one of the things that has given me snags [mental health issues] so I'm not that comfortable talking about it. It's a difficult one.

I came home, back to the Fire Service. I was lucky. I had lots of ex-servicemen colleagues and they understood, so the transition was easier than if I had been working in an office or a garage, for example. I stayed in the reserves. My intention was to do a tour every three years, Afghan came up and I had the choice of going with my own unit or waiting a year and going with 1 Staffords. I decided to go with my own unit. I understand now it was because I just wanted to get back out there. I'd missed it. I didn't know it at the time but I wanted to put myself back in danger. We did force protection at Bastion, and worked alongside the RAF regiment and the US Marines.

During that tour I injured my ankle. I noticed changes in my ankle early on, but I thought, It'll be OK, I'll just get on with it. Then I started to get these protrusions out the side of my ankle. I still carried on. I was a platoon sergeant and so my blokes were more important than I was. I guess if I had reported it earlier it might not have got so bad, but I just got on with it and decided to get it sorted back in the UK.

We were due to go out on a four-day patrol and I could hardly walk. My company second-in-command ordered me to the medical centre and, having only two weeks left, I was med-evaced out of theatre.

I had lots of physio, three operations but the ankle ended up getting fused and now it's all pinned. So I couldn't be a soldier or a firefighter any more. I was medically discharged from both in 2012. It was a massive change. In 2009 during the preparations for Afghan I was the fittest I'd ever been. Now my ankle and early degenerative changes in other joints affected both my career and my lifestyle. I loved fitness, jet-skiing, water-skiing, but that all had to stop.

I was determined not to sit around and feel sorry for myself so I did a lot of courses gearing me up to become an instructor, things like fire safety and first aid. Instructing was something I had really enjoyed in both the Army and the Fire Service. But then a job opportunity came up with the Sea Fishing Authority as a freelance auditor, auditing their instructors delivering safety training to fisherman. I went for it. I covered the whole of the UK. I set up my own business, had a team of guys working for me, it was going really well.

Then my marriage broke down. I moved out of the family house into a one-bedroom flat, trying to run a business. Then others close to me started to notice things about me that were changing. I started sinking. I went to see the GP and luckily he had recently had some kind of communication from Combat Stress. He told me I needed to contact them.

I did. Things got worse and I had to stop working. I closed the business down in 2013 and that's the last time I worked.

I was at Combat Stress receiving treatment and another client there told me about the benefits of being a member of the Band of Brothers through Help for Heroes. At that time I didn't feel that my injuries were worthy of their help. My mind-set was that the guys who had lost limbs needed support far more than me. But I was convinced to sign up to Band of Brothers, and then I got an email explaining what Turn to Starboard do. I thought they might be able to help me get back out on the water, something I had always enjoyed. I rang Tamsin and I was invited down to do the voyage with *Spirit* to the Scilly Isles. After a couple of days on the boat, my shoulders dropped and I felt more relaxed than I had for a very long time. I discovered that the sea is the environment I know I can relax in.

11

HOMEWARD BOUND

'The boy stood on the burning deck'

Felicia Hemans, 'Casabianca'

AT 1400 *SPIRIT* SLIPPED HER LINES. Everyone had enjoyed Liverpool. To have sailed so far and been able to keep this engagement was a real feeling of success. *Spirit* had done her job, and now she needed to get the crew home safe for a well-deserved pat on the back. Even though there were a fair few more miles to cover and a few more places to visit, it felt like this was the beginning of the end of the adventure. *Spirit* continued down to the Island of Anglesey, just on the eastern side of a small bay called Moelfre, dropping anchor at 2200. The fog had started to come in and as the sea was getting up a bit it was decided to anchor there for the night.

Mike, the owner and skipper of *Quivira II*, had been called away for personal reasons, so Dan had crossed over to the beautiful Rustler to help sail her. During the sail to Anglesey her engine had been intermittent so they had kept the engine off and sailed on to a buoy just over from *Spirit*, followed by *September*. Tony went over first thing in the morning to see what the problem was. Apparently it was diesel bug, a nasty little microbe that seems to adore the environment of a diesel engine and multiplies at a tremendous rate, not living that long but leaving a lot of gunk behind. The guys spent a while cleaning the little buggers out and next day everyone was all good to go.

Anglesey was the home of the mysterious Druids of the Celts, those white-robed leaders of Celtic Britain. Generally they are considered monks but they also fulfilled most of the professional class roles in medicine, law and politics. Apart from the odd human sacrifice, it was from here that they pretty much oversaw the import of gold from Ireland for distribution into Wales and further on to England. The Romans were busy spreading their own brand of freedom and turning Celtic Britain into Roman Britain, which the Druids were fully against, and they spent a lot of time whipping up the locals getting them to fight the invaders. The Romans took a strong stance on this ancient form of terrorism and so, after a few failed attempts, attacked the island, killed everybody and burnt the place to the ground.

For *Spirit* and the crew it was the last major land mass before entering the Irish Sea, the body of water that stretches all the way to the Isle of Scilly. As *Spirit* cleared land and headed out to the open waters, the weather came in, the winds picked up and the waves crashed against her from all sides.

Nothing had prepared the crew for what was to come in the next two days. Normally there is some kind of pattern, a roll that the sea and the ship agree on. It enables the crew, and more importantly their stomachs, to learn the pattern and adjust. But here with the various tides and currents all battling against each other, the only pattern was chaos. A lot of the crew suffered greatly, but luckily not all together. By some kind of miracle the staggered periods of sickness enabled *Spirit* to carry on. She, of course, was fine, crashing through the waves as happily now as she had done for many years.

The instruction was given for people to stay below. The waves and the constant rolling made the deck a suitable place only for those persons essential to the sailing of the ship. Almost to a person, everyone agreed that this had been the most punishing part. When *Spirit* got past South Bishop at the northern end of St Brides Bay in Pembrokeshire, South Wales, and into the simpler elements of the Atlantic swells, it was a huge relief. Everyone got a phone signal, so it was great for chatting to family and letting them know about the plans and the timings, and that everyone was OK, if a bit green.

The smaller yachts had decided to hug the coast, to keep out of the jaws of the weather. They were going to bypass the Scillies and find a suitable rendezvous point for all to meet up later on. When the Scillies finally came into view it was as if *Spirit* was a ship from the Age of Discovery, finally sighting land after months at sea. A pod of dolphins came over to say hello, darting and diving at the bow, turning to the side and looking up at the motley bunch of sailors entering this scenic place. Then came a real highlight, a school of whales, their blowholes spitting vapour high out of the water.

'Thar she blows,' Russ cried, unable to resist.

What a wonderful welcome.

For the last seven weeks Tamsin had been repeating the same phrase: 'Wait till you get to the Scillies. It's the most beautiful place in the world.'

On 26 July, at 0900, *Spirit*'s crew dropped the anchor in New Grimsby Harbour on the island of Tresco, Scillies. Ahead of schedule and needing some respite after the gruelling Irish Sea, the Scillies provided a perfect place to relax. After a couple of briefings and checking that everything on board was shipshape, it was off for a wander and a nose around. Shaun's son was there to welcome him, a wonderful family moment for both of them.

The Scillies, on a latitude of 6 degrees west, are the most westerly part of the UK. The population are justly proud of this and it manifests itself in T-shirts and baseball caps displaying the coordinates; the crew certainly bought a few. There are five inhabited islands and a few that are uninhabited. As you might imagine, the islands have a huge maritime history. One of the most influential events in British naval history, or even world maritime history, happened here in the 1700s. In 1707 the Navy had been unsuccessfully attacking Toulon in France as part of a combined force to destroy part of the French fleet. It wasn't very effective so it was sent home. It was quite an armada: twenty-one ships in total, and four ships of the line, which was the name for the larger warships with rows and rows of cannons that they used to broadside each other. The guy in charge was an experienced and respected Admiral of the Fleet named Sir Cloudesley Shovell.

They believed they were passing an island called Ushant that lies off Brittany, but thanks to a major miscalculation they were actually approaching the Scillies. By the time they realised this, four ships had already struck rock. It was one of the worst disasters ever to befall the fleet. About 1,500 died, and their bodies washed up on the beaches for days. In those times, shipwrecks were quite a positive event for the local people, and the bodies would have been searched for anything to help the plight of the living rather than mourn the dead.

A story emerged later in the century that prior to the shipwreck a common sailor, a local to the islands, had recognised the waters and raised doubts with his officers about where they claimed to be. For his troubles they strung him up and hanged him from the yardarm.

What this disaster put in motion was a process to solve the biggest issue in navigation. No sailor was able to calculate longitude effectively. They used dead reckoning, a rudimentary method of determining your position using bearing and distance travelled. In the investigations and court martials that followed the Scillies disaster, quite a few miscalculations came to light, bringing the longitude problem to a head. In 1714, the government passed the Longitude Act, which offered a reward for anyone who could solve it. The solution was to come from a very unusual source: Yorkshire carpenter and watchmaker John Harrison. He obsessed over the problem, building huge prototypes and sailing them on naval ships. It took thirty years before Harrison created what is now called the H4, a giant pocket watch that kept almost perfect time at sea. It enabled mariners to know exactly what the time was in Greenwich and therefore, by adding on the astronomical calculations, to establish exactly where they were. It was a huge success. Captain Cook, the Whitby-based discoverer extraordinaire, had one in his possession during his Southern Ocean exploits.

Even William Bligh, captain of the *Bounty*, the ship that was famous for its mutiny, was given one. The inciter of the mutiny, Fletcher Christian, might well have burnt the ship when they reached the Pitcairn Islands but he certainly kept Harrison's H4. It now sits in the Royal Observatory in Greenwich, a suitable home.

Another sensible action would be to erect a lighthouse, but one wasn't completed in the Scillies until 1858. It has since had many incarnations, and today a traditional-looking lighthouse warns sailors where they are.

Spirit moved her anchor so the crew could visit other parts of the islands and visit some of Tamsin's various favourite spots. It would seem she had quite a few.

'Now, this is definitely my favourite!' she would say.

After dropping off some of the guys to go and take advantage of free tickets to the local health spa, Chris returned to *Spirit* and tied up the tender to one of the stations, then wandered down below. For some reason, he felt something wasn't right. He went back on deck to quell his uneasy feeling. Floating away, free as a bird, was the tender. Chris had obviously not tied it secure enough.

There was nothing else for it but to strip off and swim to retrieve it, much to the entertainment of those still on board. Another kangaroo court was called to session that evening. The penalty was to tie a bowline knot every hour on the hour and to have it checked by Dan.

Everyone was relaxing, enjoying the wonderful beaches and contemplating what was to come next. *Quivira* and *September* had gone on to the mainland and were in the harbour at Newlyn, the famous old fishing town of Cornwall. They had tried to get into Penzance but there was no room. Newlyn is still a thriving fishing village, but at one time it was the herring capital of the British Isles.

After visiting so many fishing ports around the country and seeing statues and boards that explained the once great days of the herring industry, it seemed time to find out more about it. The herring is a relatively small fish, silver in colour, which gave it many nicknames: 'the silver of the sea' being one, the hints of wealth quite deliberate since this little oily critter was a great source of income. Almost all European countries fished them and enjoyed various ways of preparing them. In the UK the most famous would be the kipper, a whole smoked herring.

The 1800s was boom-time for the Cornish coastline fishing communities. The herring would arrive in the summer months and huge schools would be found not too far off the southern coast. Using large drift nets, hundreds of boats would get the catch back to the port as quickly as possible. As such an oily fish, it went off quickly. Once into harbour the men would turn their catch over to the herring girls, who'd work in threes, two gutting and one packing. They salted the fish to preserve them, but the salt would attack the skin of their hands. In an attempt to protect their hands, they would bandage them. It was piecework, so speed was key. Incredibly, the herring girls kept up an average of one herring a second throughout 15-hour shifts, all going into barrels to be despatched to the awaiting markets on the continent.

Inadvertently *Spirit* had been travelling an A–Z of the major herring ports. Wick in Scotland had a new port built in 1811 by the British Fishery Society. Tobermory on the Isle of Mull and Stornoway on the Isle of Lewis also had industries based around the 'silver darling'. When the herring shoals migrated south during the summer months, the herring girls would travel the east coast to follow work. Sometimes as many as 2,500 would leave Stornoway and gut fish all the way down to Great Yarmouth.

Newlyn was the centre of the Cornish part of the business. This tough fishing community got a reputation as quite a challenging place to live. The herring girls must have taken some serious wooing.

The good times, as they always do, came to an end. The harbours of the UK started to lose out to large fishing boats, some from overseas, some home-grown. The fish still got caught but it wasn't by the boat-owning fishermen any more.

In all these wonderful communities, there are still fishermen. Newlyn has a thriving fishing business, its fish market is one of the best in the county, but it's not herring any more.

The First World War strained the relationship between British herrings and the healthy industry exporting the fish to Germany, where it was a very popular dish at the time. All the fishermen were drafted into the Navy and their boats, lying unused, slowly rotted.

Tamsin's Story

I was born in North Cornwall, in a place called Landrake, and I moved to Falmouth when I was a few months old. Cornwall is such a great place to grow up, a perfect playground. The sea and being on boats is as much part of my life as being on land. My younger sister and I were brought up on Cornish pasties, the sea and sunshine. My grandad had a boat, *Shenanigan*. He was Irish and we'd fly a spinnaker in the colours of the Irish flag. You couldn't miss us! I spent time on that boat since I was ten weeks old. It was as normal for me as sitting in my bedroom. Family holidays were always sailing, France or the Scillies.

Sailing and music have both been a huge part of my life. I love being part of a team and having a common goal, whether it's as part of the crew on a boat or part of a full orchestra. I went on to study music at university, including a semester in Paris at the Sorbonne.

When I was 12 years old I got involved with the Falmouth Sail Training Ship. They have a 50-foot ketch *Hardiesse* and they nurtured young sailors. I learnt so much from them.

Through my time sailing on *Hardiesse* I knew I wanted to sail on the larger tall ships. In 2008 I was lucky enough to get a place on the Funchal 500 Tall

Ships Regatta, sailing from Falmouth to Portugal. I then continued regularly to crew on tall ships for the next six years, becoming experienced enough to sail as a watch leader and lead others during the voyage. I had amazing opportunities during this time, completing two transatlantic passages and many miles around the UK, Northern Europe, Scandinavia and the Caribbean.

By the summer of 2014 I had finished my degree and returned home to Falmouth. I took a last-minute volunteer opportunity to sail on TS *Pelican* as a watch leader from Falmouth to Greenwich for the Tall Ships Regatta. There is something quite special about leaving from your home port for a voyage.

It was here that I met Shaun. He had chartered TS *Pelican* for the regatta for Turn to Starboard, and had brought together twenty-nine veterans and serving personnel for the voyage. As someone with limited military connections and background, I was a little apprehensive about leading and teaching such an experienced team — even though they were not sailors — but I had nothing to worry about. The trip proved to be a perfect introduction to the military. The only thing I had to worry about was laughing too much!

During the voyage Shaun told me more about Turn to Starboard and I was hooked. I loved the concept and the impact he was having, and it felt like joining a family. Turn to Starboard was growing rapidly at that time, was just about to sign for office premises and there was talk of the potential gift of the 92-foot schooner *Spirit of Fairbridge* from The Prince's Trust. At the end of the voyage Shaun offered me some work with Turn to Starboard, and I accepted. A few weeks later, Shaun and I met in our new offices, just us and two chairs. How things have changed since then!

Shaun had always wanted to do a significant voyage with *Spirit* when we got her. A challenge and a real adventure. We wanted to keep this local to the UK and loved the idea of sailing her round Britain. Although originally planned for 2015, the charity at that time was still growing rapidly and we delayed for a year so we didn't overstretch our resources.

Once we had recruited our crew and set the dates, we set about the huge task of preparing for the adventure. We planned to sail anti-clockwise around Britain, beginning and ending in Falmouth, taking eight weeks for the voyage.

I didn't know when I began at Turn to Starboard how special the job would turn out to be. I've had weeks where I'll spend one day crouched in an engine bilge with a pocket full of spanners, and the next sipping tea at Buckingham Palace. It is the people who make it, though. I've learnt so much from them and continue to do so every day. Sailing and working at Turn to Starboard feels like having thirty naughty and very protective big brothers around all the time. I had always wanted an older brother when I was little, so it looks like I got what I wished for!

12

FALMOUTH

'If I had been around when Rubens was painting, I would have been revered as a fabulous model. Kate Moss? Well, she would have been the paintbrush'

Dawn French

AND THEN WITHOUT TOO MUCH FUSS it was time to sail back to Falmouth, the home of *Spirit* and the charity Turn to Starboard. *Spirit* was to arrive on the first of August, two months after she left. Chris was leading this leg and started plotting his way points, working out tides and bearings. The anchor was raised and the magical Scillies started to grow smaller and smaller as *Spirit* continued east and past Wolf Rock, a particularly nasty rock sticking up out of the water, which now politely has a lighthouse.

The mood on the boat was akin to a feeling most soldiers have experienced and certainly it was mentioned many times aboard.

'This is just like coming back off tour,' Chris said, and most agreed.

There is moment on a tour when the date of getting out approaches and it's natural to let your mind wander, to think of loved ones, of favourite meals, of lie-ins, of anything that has been impossible in theatre. It's a dangerous moment, because the reality of the last six months isn't about to change and the enemy isn't going to give you a few easy days just because you're off home soon. It's time, if anything, to be more vigilant.

The crew weren't quite that intense, but the sea is both friend and enemy and keeping a high level of awareness was a good idea. Chris's passage went without any hiccups. The plan was to meet up with *Quivira II* and *September* in the Helford River, home waters, a place everyone knew as it was a favoured place to do sail-training. One of the small creeks that make up the river is Frenchman's Creek, the setting of the Daphne du Maurier book about a lady of means falling in love with a French pirate, giving hope to pirates everywhere.

Spirit would be getting in last as she had more distance to cover. The two smaller yachts arrived a day earlier, and at 1900 *Spirit* dropped anchor for the last time on the challenge. Her next stop would be Falmouth, where she'd be back in her usual spot in the marina.

As if the feeling of being nearly home wasn't enough, all three crews were treated to a most incredible sunset, the sun slowly sinking behind the Lizard before warming up the locals on another part of the globe. A somewhat poetic, poignant moment. It was 31 July. The next day was the last day, the final leg. Everyone got together on *Spirit* to share this final moment, cooking together, laughing together. So many friendships had been built between the crew. Everyone had had their moments but had seen them through.

From Helford to Falmouth in sailing terms is a small hop, a hop that everyone was fairly familiar with. It was a nice, calm, late start, to get everyone in on time for a midday arrival. But even seeing the word 'Falmouth' written in the log couldn't convince us that, yes, it was nearly over.

We left the mouth of the river and passed August Rock, then sailed towards Falmouth harbour, passing the beaches of Maenporth and Swanspool and approaching the Pendennis Fort, high on the point, built to protect the coast from the Spanish marauders back when cannons were *de rigueur*. We sailed past the huge café restaurant on Gillyvase beach, already busy with clients sipping their cappuccinos and looking out at the three boats drifting past, none the wiser about the adventure we had been on. Then past Black Rock, which appears on the Falmouth town coat-of-arms, forever warning sailors to beware the nasty surprises that can await you under the waves. The Governor was the last westerly marker before we headed into the harbour proper.

Chris and Yanto got their harnesses on to climb the rigging in order to wave as the ship came around the point.

'We should just carry on and do it again,' Russ said. Everyone laughed, thinking the same.

Spirit's permanent berth came into view. A throng of people were on the quayside, waving and cheering. The Turn to Starboard team were there, families were there, people who had completed part but not all of the journey were there. As *Spirit* slowly and elegantly pulled alongside, everyone was relieved, sad, happy – a huge mixture of emotions, but there was a smile on everyone's face.

It had taken two months. Now *Spirit* and her crew were home.

Clive handed Shaun a bottle of champagne, which he dutifully opened, spraying the crew like he was a Formula One winner. He also had a blow-up whale under his arms and threw that on to the deck.

'There is more chance of a whale landing on the deck than being struck by lightning,' he said.

Dan laughed. 'I love it that you've gone to so much trouble to call me a nobber.'

The press were there and a few guys did interviews. Words flowed but no one could remember what they said afterwards, except that it was all good.

The local pub Five Degrees was putting on a welcome home party. While friends and families hugged, the guys finished up on deck, showered and wandered up the road to the pub to join them. The food at the pub was being dutifully demolished. The food on the voyage had been surprising good, but pasties are a delicacy in these parts.

You could tell who the crew were. They had suntans, were a fair few pounds lighter and wore their Round Britain grey fleeces with damn-well-earned pride. Shaun stood up to say a few words. He had spoken so emotionally on the day of departure, and now there were a few teases but he couldn't contain his happiness. He spoke well and held the crowd, thanking the many people who had contributed, large or small. It had taken a huge amount of effort to put this trip on.

In every way it had far exceeded its original goal, which was to help veterans acquire sea miles and experience on the way to becoming yachtmasters. Throughout the trip local press had taken interest, writing articles and spreading the word, letting people know that good things, nay, great things, are still possible for those veterans suffering from readjustment to civilian life.

It had made a huge difference to people's self-belief. The crew had weathered so many challenges and could proudly say they completed a real, proper, seafaring, a once-in-a-lifetime adventure. There are magical things happening in Falmouth. Turn to Starboard is helping people get their lives back. If you know anyone who is struggling in any way with the effects of life after the military, put them in touch with this wonderful charity.

Spirit will be doing this again in 2017. She will need new faces to help, nurture and protect.

It cast me back to that cold wintery Sunday when I had that knowledgeable visitor, one from her past.

'People forget we are an island and therefore a sailing nation. We should never forget those skills, and I'm so pleased she is still helping people.'

So are we.

AFTERWORD

DAN IS MAKING FALMOUTH his new home. He still works for Turn to Starboard and continues to flourish, coaching other beneficiaries to follow in his footsteps.

Tamsin continues to be incredible, having her amazing contribution recognised by being made one of Cornwall's Top 30 under 30. There will certainly be more awards to come.

Rich is giving *Spirit* all the love she deserves and is getting her ready for another adventure, while still covering all the other roles.

Clive has left the forces after thirty-nine years and is starting a new job in the civilian world. Good luck to him.

Adrian has completed his yachtmaster theory and is on track to getting his ticket.

Al moved into a new flat and is doing well down in Falmouth, getting miles and training for his qualification.

Chris hurt his back on Boxing Day while innocently lifting a box out of his car, and that put him out of sailing for a while. He promises to be on the waves as soon as he recovers.

Yanto felt that just sailing around Britain wasn't enough. He decided to fly around as well. He did so late last year and visited all the haunts again. He now plans to drive it together with Chris to raise more money for charity.

Russ has completed his degree and is keeping everyone entertained as a radio DJ.

Tony moved back to his home in Saltash and is getting on with being the fixer.

Shaun continues to run one of the most inspirational organisations in existence. Turn to Starboard is growing every day, yet Shaun always has the patience to spend time with people.

As for me, I wrote this book as an attempt to tell these stories, doing a bit of movie extra work when I can. Now, after months of typing, I can get back on the water.

ABOUT TURN TO STARBOARD

IT IS EASY TO FALL INTO A well-ploughed furrow of describing charities in glowing terms; military sympathy is running high at the present, certainly with those who have served far more than those who send.

However, on this occasion there is something very magical and special about the charity Turn to Starboard. I had wanted to include Shaun's story as part of the background but he in his usual modest manner declined and wished only that I explain what the charity is about, I feel the best way to do this is to show what it has done to date, in 2016.

THE MISSION

Turn to Starboard uses RYA sailing courses to support Armed Forces personnel, retired and serving, affected by military operations and the unique nature of Service life, focusing on re-integration, re-engagement and providing tangible experiences, expert training and career building opportunities, all in a supportive and unique environment.

THE IMPACT

427 sailing opportunities in 2016

141 sailing opportunities on board *Spirit of Falmouth*

84 skill building and milege week places for the Zero to Hero Yachtmaster participants

80 RAF ST Mawgan family members attended the family engagement and sailing taster days on *Spirit*

47 RYA Competent Crew and Day Skipper opportunities

33 family members sailed with us

30 participants on our Zero to Hero Yachtmaster programme

12 shorebased course opportunities.

www.turntostarboard.co.uk

ACKNOWLEDGEMENTS

I'M NEVER SURE IF THIS PART OF a book is ever read, certainly not by people who weren't involved. So I might be tempted to slip in song lyrics or the odd bit of literary nonsense.

I always think this is the writer's version of the Oscar speech, where the teary-eyed recipient stands up and lists the names of people you've never heard of, cracking private jokes to those who probably wrote, dressed, filmed, edited, promoted, fetched coffee, fed, dropped dry cleaning off, looked after the kids, put up with antics, and got paid an absolute pittance.

Well, let's say I'm the diva here and the people here are the poor souls who got roped into helping with this book.

Above all I would like to thank Imogen, who had the ordeal of being with me throughout the journey of both the trip and the book, keeping my spirits high when they sagged. Thank you so much. This book is as much yours as mine.

Damaris, Rachel and Aidan for giving me support in the first place and telling me I can write. Hannah for having the confidence to put me in touch with her book contacts.

Janet, Henry, Mari and Lizzy at Bloomsbury who made a daunting thing quite palatable.

Pat, Dennis, Darren, David, Martyn and all those others in the veterans' recovery arena who tirelessly spend their time listening to me whine yet have the patience to help men like me become useful again.

Help for Heroes, ABF The Soldiers Charity, Veteran's Aid, Combat Stress, Royal British Legion. Thank you.

I have a lot of good friends. For a while I forgot that and luckily I now have them back.

Dean and Dom for understanding about our experiences and getting me home.

Lydia for always giving me safe place to hide from the world.

All from 6 platoon, who know that however long it is we don't speak, there is always a bond.

The guys from Cohort 65/66 who love a pond swim as much as me.

Some key people whose involvement in the project made this happen but who wanted to keep their privacy.

This is not an account of my trip, it is an account of all the crew. I have to thank all of them for putting up with the multiple phone calls from me to check and double-check things, for their honesty in sharing their own personal stories in full graphic detail, knowing that they would go out into wide world.

To all the local people in Cornwall who welcomed me with such open arms and allowed me to finally find a home after many years of wandering.

To those at Turn to Starboard, the staff and volunteers who have quite honestly kept me alive and kept me from being another sad statistic.

To Mike for lending his Rustler *Quivira II* for guys to sail on when the numbers became to many for just *Spirit of Falmouth*. It's like lending a Rolls Royce for a road journey.

I have met many people since getting involved with this project. Some came with us on the trip, some couldn't make it, some found it too much of a challenge, but all have inspired me. It's quite humbling to spend time with people who have had huge obstacles to overcome before they can even think of things like happiness and contentment.

And all of this is down to one thing and one thing only: the generosity of the British public, who in the period that I have been involved with both military actions and its aftermath have been nothing but incredible in showing that they do care about their soldiers and the old adage, often attributed to George Orwell:

'People sleep peaceably in their beds, because rough men threaten violence on their behalf.'